THE
1-DAY
MARKETING
PLAN

THE
1-DAY
MARKETING
PLAN

*Organizing and Completing
the Plan that Works*

Roman G. Hiebing, Jr.
Scott W. Cooper

Printed on recyclable paper

NTC Business Books
a division of *NTC Publishing Group* • Lincolnwood, Illinois USA

Library of Congress Cataloging-in-Publication Data

Hiebing, Roman G.
    The 1-day marketing plan: organizing and completing the right plan for your
company / Roman G. Hiebing, Jr., Scott W. Cooper.
        p. cm.
    Includes index.
    ISBN 0-8442-3358-7 (hardcover); 0-8442-3359-5 (softcover)
    1. Marketing—Management. 2. Strategic planning. I. Cooper, Scott W.
    II. Title.
HF5415.13.H53   1992
658.8 02—dc20   91-35192
                                                                           CIP

1996 Printing

Published by National Textbook Company, a division of NTC Publishing Group.
4255 West Touhy Avenue, Lincolnwood (Chicago), Illinois 60646-1975 U.S.A.

Manufactured in the United States of America.

6 7 8 9 BC 9 8 7 6 5 4 3

Foreword

Marketing planning has been critical to the success and growth of our business over the past 15 years. And I think it will become absolutely essential to businesses during the very competitive '90s. Those businesses that are effective in this area will survive and prosper. Those that aren't, won't.

Famous Footwear has been fortunate to work with Roman and Scott for over 15 years. During that time they have assisted us in the development of yearly plans for our more than 350 stores as well as worked with us in developing countless individual market and individual store-level marketing plans. I am a big believer in basic marketing plans, whether it is for one small business, a single store or a major corporation. In my business, the day-to-day executional demands can be so overwhelming that without the overall direction a plan brings, it is very difficult to keep all the parts moving in the same direction. Marketing plans give my company that short-term *and* long-term direction. Yet we cannot afford to waste half the year planning. We need to move and move very quickly.

Marketing planning can take a lot of valuable time and the process can waste a lot of time if there is not an effective structure and road map to follow. This book will help save you time by providing the structure you need to write a marketing plan. Too many businesses find themselves making decisions on guesses and hunches or going in different directions. The disciplined marketing planning process outlined in this book forces the marketer to make decisions based upon facts and not guesses. More importantly, the book provides a sequential step-by-step guide to completing a truly integrated plan. When you are finished you don't have just an advertising plan, just a promotion plan or just a pricing plan—but an integrated marketing plan that will work because all the pieces fit together.

If you follow Roman and Scott's marketing plan process, you will not only save a tremendous amount of time, you'll prepare a better marketing plan—that works!

Brian Cook
President
Famous Footwear
The Brown Group, Inc.

Contents

STEP THREE

Sales Objectives

STEP FOUR

Target Market

STEP FIVE

**Marketing Objectives
and Strategies**

STEP EIGHT

Marketing Plan Budget and Calendar

STEP NINE

Execution

STEP TEN

Evaluation

18

Introduction

The purpose of this book is to provide you with a practical step-by-step guide for preparing your own marketing plan. This is not a discussion of marketing theory, but a book with real world answers to help you meet head-on specific marketing challenges, whatever your level of marketing expertise or the size and type of your organization.

The book is organized to keep you focused on addressing the necessary major and minor steps in the marketing planning process. This book provides the reader with a disciplined and integrated approach to marketing planning: a tested approach that will help you develop an effective, target market driven marketing plan in one day. You will also find that this book will keep you on track, eliminate wasted effort, and, most importantly, help you utilize a planning process that has achieved results for companies both large and small—from *Fortune* 500 to entrepreneurial start-ups.

WHAT THE READER CAN EXPECT

This book provides a comprehensive approach to marketing planning—from describing what background information is necessary and how to analyze it, to writing the marketing plan specifics and evaluating the executional results of the plan. Whatever the marketing challenge, this how-to approach will have direct application because it is based on proven marketing principles and hundreds of real business experiences. A wide variety of actual examples, drawn from the authors' experiences, have been included to help the reader understand the marketing principles and the step-by-step marketing plan development process.

This book focuses primarily on the most important part of any marketing program—the *preparation of a marketing plan*, not its implementation. It includes helpful planning and research tools; it does *not* dwell on specific execution. The authors have found that if a marketer makes the required effort to prepare an effective marketing plan, arriving at the actual executional elements is the easy part—they flow naturally from the strategic framework of the marketing plan. In our opinion, far too often marketing failures are the result of marketing executions that were *not* rooted in a well-thought-out marketing plan prepared in a disciplined fashion.

DISCIPLINED MARKETING PLANNING

The key to writing an effective marketing plan is disciplined marketing planning. However, before defining disciplined marketing planning, it is necessary first to describe what is a _marketing plan._ We define a marketing plan as an arranged structure to guide the process of determining the target market for your product or service, detailing the target market's needs and wants, and then fulfilling these needs and wants better than the competition.

Disciplined marketing planning is a sequential, interlocking, step-by-step decision and action process. In using this disciplined approach, you follow a 10-step logical process that allows you to define issues, answer questions correctly, and make decisions. Each major step, as depicted by a box on the disciplined marketing planning chart in Exhibit 1, should be completed before going on to the next. Further, each major step is broken down into individual, ordered, minor steps providing a clear and efficient road map for preparing an effective fully integrated marketing plan.

The disciplined approach, although initially more demanding, dramatically increases the chances of your product's or service's success, because the marketing plan prepared in this manner is just that—totally planned. It is a databased plan that is very encompassing yet feasible to execute.

HOW THE PLANNING PROCESS WORKS

Disciplined marketing planning has two major components. The first, marketing background, includes the business review, commonly referred to as a situation analysis, and the problems and opportunities segment. The business review is a comprehensive analysis of the marketplace and of your own organization broken down into sequentially ordered sections; the problem and opportunities segment is a summary of challenges emerging from the business review. The second major component is the marketing plan itself, which is developed from the information gathered and analyzed in the marketing background section. The marketing plan is totally inclusive and can be prepared in one day if the marketing background segment has been developed in a comprehensive manner. The marketing plan begins in sequential order with the sales objectives and ends with a budget and calendar of marketing activities necessary to realize the sales objectives. This disciplined method also allows you to build testing programs into the final marketing plan.

Once the plan is prepared, it must be executed and then evaluated. Although evaluation is the last step in the process, with it begins anew the whole disciplined approach, because evaluation becomes a major part of the background section in the preparation of next year's marketing plan. In this easy-to-use book, each element within the marketing background and plan sections, along with the evaluation process, is discussed in summary fashion. If you desire a more detailed discussion of the disciplined marketing planning process, along with a unique "Idea Starters by Marketing Situation" grid with over 1,000 different idea combinations, you can refer to _How to Write a Successful Marketing Plan,_ also written by the authors of this book and published by NTC Business Books.

EXHIBIT 1   Ten Steps to Disciplined Marketing Planning

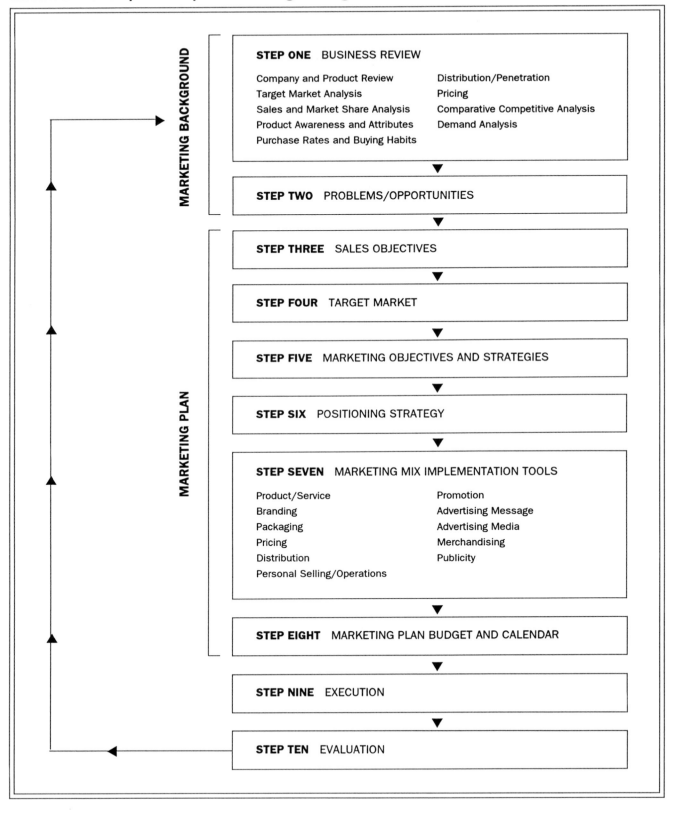

MARKETING BACKGROUND

STEP ONE   BUSINESS REVIEW

Company and Product Review	Distribution/Penetration
Target Market Analysis	Pricing
Sales and Market Share Analysis	Comparative Competitive Analysis
Product Awareness and Attributes	Demand Analysis
Purchase Rates and Buying Habits	

STEP TWO   PROBLEMS/OPPORTUNITIES

MARKETING PLAN

STEP THREE   SALES OBJECTIVES

STEP FOUR   TARGET MARKET

STEP FIVE   MARKETING OBJECTIVES AND STRATEGIES

STEP SIX   POSITIONING STRATEGY

STEP SEVEN   MARKETING MIX IMPLEMENTATION TOOLS

Product/Service	Promotion
Branding	Advertising Message
Packaging	Advertising Media
Pricing	Merchandising
Distribution	Publicity
Personal Selling/Operations	

STEP EIGHT   MARKETING PLAN BUDGET AND CALENDAR

STEP NINE   EXECUTION

STEP TEN   EVALUATION

HOW TO USE THIS BOOK IN MARKETING PLANNING

We recommend that before you begin writing your marketing plan, you read through the entire book to understand the complete process and all that goes into preparing a comprehensive marketing plan. Next, as you actually prepare your own marketing plan, go through each chapter that applies to your situation again and very diligently attempt to follow the step-by-step disciplined marketing planning process as presented in this book.

As you use the disciplined marketing planning process, keep in mind that while you should understand the basic marketing principles provided throughout this book and follow the recommended methodology, you can adapt the review and planning process to best fit your product or marketing situation as well as time requirements. Remember that you want to be open-minded and innovative but also methodical and consistent as you prepare the marketing background section and write the marketing plan.

As you go through the whole process, you will come up with all types of ideas and testing opportunities for different areas of the actual marketing plan that might not relate to the specific section of the plan you are currently writing. Don't lose these ideas, because they will be very helpful when you prepare the particular section to which they apply. As you prepare the background section and the marketing plan itself, have separate sheets of paper handy with headings of problems, opportunities, and each step of the marketing plan (including a separate sheet of paper for each marketing mix tool) under which you can jot down relevant ideas as they occur to you. Don't evaluate the worth of each idea as you think of it, but jot it down. Evaluate its application as you actually write the section of the marketing plan to which it pertains.

Also keep in mind that many of the principles, procedures, and examples provided in this book will have application to your particular marketing situation even though it has not been written just for your specific product or service. In fact, this book is written for broad application by marketers of consumer/package goods products, business-to-business products, services, or retail outlets with private, public, or nonprofit organizations. For simplicity and brevity, however, the word *product* is usually used throughout this book in generic planning discussions for whatever is to be marketed. When there is specific reference to consumer or business-to-business products, services, or retail, it will be singled out accordingly.

STEP ONE | Business Review

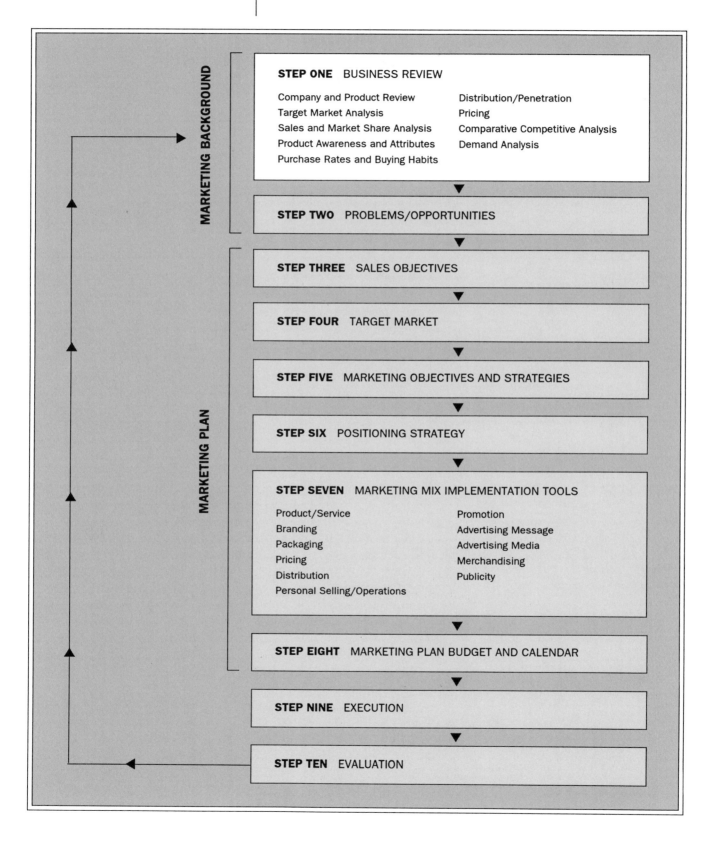

MARKETING BACKGROUND

STEP ONE BUSINESS REVIEW

Company and Product Review	Distribution/Penetration
Target Market Analysis	Pricing
Sales and Market Share Analysis	Comparative Competitive Analysis
Product Awareness and Attributes	Demand Analysis
Purchase Rates and Buying Habits	

STEP TWO PROBLEMS/OPPORTUNITIES

MARKETING PLAN

STEP THREE SALES OBJECTIVES

STEP FOUR TARGET MARKET

STEP FIVE MARKETING OBJECTIVES AND STRATEGIES

STEP SIX POSITIONING STRATEGY

STEP SEVEN MARKETING MIX IMPLEMENTATION TOOLS

Product/Service	Promotion
Branding	Advertising Message
Packaging	Advertising Media
Pricing	Merchandising
Distribution	Publicity
Personal Selling/Operations	

STEP EIGHT MARKETING PLAN BUDGET AND CALENDAR

STEP NINE EXECUTION

STEP TEN EVALUATION

The Business Review

DEFINITION

The business review provides a quantitative and qualitative decision making base for the subsequent marketing plan and a rationale for all strategic marketing decisions within the plan.

Marketing is a broad discipline in which multiple decisions must be made—decisions such as which potential customers should be targeted, through what specific combination of product features, with what price, through what distribution channels, with what type of service, via what type of communication, and at what time of year. However, these decisions cannot be made without a systematic review of all known facts. The business review provides these facts so that sound decision making can be achieved.

OVERVIEW

This section is intended to organize your work on the business review you develop in Chapter 2. Following these suggestions will save time and help create a more effective database from which to make decisions.

In order to complete the 1-day marketing plan, the marketer should start the business review process 2–3 weeks prior to actually writing the marketing plan. You will then be assured that you have the information needed to write the plan. If this is not possible, go directly to Chapter 2 and answer the questions at the end of each of the 10 business review steps. Answer the questions from a "directional" standpoint. Remember, it is not important whether your market share is 15 percent or 17 percent. What is important is whether your market share has been increasing or decreasing relative to other key competitors. This is what is meant by directional—the concept is critical in developing an actionable, effective, 1-day marketing plan.

A well-developed business review should be utilized as a daily reference piece. Each year, your business review should be updated to reflect the most recent changes in your industry and company. Therefore, if this is your first business review, don't be overwhelmed. Work on those sections that most affect your business. Then, next year, update those sections and further complete some of the others that you didn't have time for previously.

Completing the business review can be more than a one-person job. Request assistance from other people in your company to help compile the information. The step-by-step process of completing the business review in Chapter 2 allows for a marketer to easily manage the information gathering process. Follow the suggestions below, paying particular attention to those steps of the business review that have greatest impact on your business.

SIX SUGGESTIONS FOR PREPARING THE BUSINESS REVIEW

Suggestion 1: Prepare an Outline

Always start by developing a written outline. The outline should be as specific as possible, covering each major area of the business review. This outline of steps to be covered in a business review helps you stay focused and ensures that critical data needed for actionable marketing plans will be obtained in a disciplined and sequential process. The outline serves as an overview for the business review questions and charts presented in Chapter 2. An example of what the outline of your own business review should look like follows.

Step 1: Corporate philosophy/description of the company and products
- A. Corporate goals and objectives
- B. General company and product history
- C. Company organization

Step 2: Review of the consumer target market
- A. Demographics and lifestyle factors
- B. Product usage
- C. Heavy users
- D. Potential primary and secondary target markets

Step 3: Review of the business-to-business target market
- A. Target market segmentation and Standard Industrial Classification (SIC) categories
- B. Base segmenting
- C. Other methods of segmenting
  1. Dollar size
  2. Number of employees
  3. Heavy usage rates
  4. Product application/use
  5. Organization structure
  6. New versus repeat buyer
  7. Geographic location
  8. Decision makers and influencers

Step 4: Sales analysis
- A. Total sales
- B. Sales by brand or department
- C. Market share

    D. Store-for-store sales for retailers

    E. Seasonality of sales

    F. Sales by geographic territory/target market segments

Step 5: Product awareness and attributes

    A. Product awareness

    B. Product attributes

Step 6: Purchase rates/buying habits

    A. Purchase rates of the product category and your company's product by geographic markets

    B. Trading areas

    C. Brand loyalty

    D. Buying habits

    E. Trial and retrial

Step 7: Distribution

    A. Retail

        1. Channel type/trends

        2. Geography

        3. Penetration

    B. Package goods

        1. Channel type/trends

        2. Market coverage

        3. Shelf space

        4. Geography

        5. Sales method

    C. Business-to-business

        1. Channel type/trends

        2. Geography

        3. Personal selling method

    D. Service firms

        1. Type of office

        2. Geography

        3. Penetration

Step 8: Pricing

    A. Price of your product

    B. Sales by price point

    C. Price elasticity

    D. Cost structure

Step 9: Historical marketing review of your company versus the competition

    A. How to develop competitive information

        1. Market share/sales

    2. Target market
    3. Marketing objectives and strategies
    4. Positioning
    5. Product/branding/packaging strengths and weaknesses
    6. Pricing
    7. Distribution/store penetration/market coverage
    8. Personal selling
    9. Promotion
    10. Advertising message
    11. Media strategy and expenditures
    12. Customer service policies
    13. Merchandising
    14. Publicity
    15. Testing/marketing R&D
  B. Summary of strengths and weaknesses

Step 10: Demand analysis
  A. Target market
  B. Geographical territory
  C. Consumption constraints
  D. Average purchase per year per customer
  E. Total purchase per year in category
  F. Average price
  G. Total dollar purchases
  H. Your company's market share
  I. Additional factors

Suggestion 2: Develop Questions

List questions to be answered for each section of the business review outline. The questions will provide direction in determining what specific information you need to accumulate.

Suggestion 3: Develop Data Charts

Develop data charts with headings to help structure your search for relevant information. When completed, the charts should help you answer the major questions included in Chapter 2 pertaining to each step of the business review outline. Organize the headings and columns of the charts first to determine what information needs to be found prior to the data search. This forces you to look for data and numbers that will provide meaningful information. Remember, if you look for data before developing your charts, you may tend to construct the charts around what is easy to find, not what should be found.

Suggestion 4: Develop Reference Points for Comparisons

Always develop charts that have reference points for comparison so that the data are actionable. If you state sales growth for your company, provide sales growth for the industry. In this manner, the company's sales growth can be judged against a reference point. And whenever possible, include five-year trend information so that the current year's performance can be judged relative to past years' performance.

Suggestion 5: Conduct a Data Search

Institute a disciplined data search. Stay focused on what needs to be found by constantly reviewing your outline. This will allow you to feel confident that you have compiled all existing data necessary to complete your charts.

Suggestion 6: Write Summary Statements

After the charts have been completed, write brief statements summarizing the major findings and answering the questions you developed in Suggestion 2. Include a summary rationale when needed. Keep it objective by strictly reporting the findings; don't provide solutions at this point. The business review is not for developing objectives and strategies. It is for providing facts from which to develop a marketing plan and to provide a rationale for that plan.

Organizing the Business Review

The sections of the final written business review should be in the same sequence as the steps developed in your outline. Each section should include summary statements followed by completed, detailed data charts. Finally, write the marketing background and plan in the third person, being as objective as possible, not interjecting your own personal feelings that cannot be documented by fact. Write in a very clear, concise manner so there can be no misinterpretation of what is presented. Don't assume that everyone who reads the plan will have the same base of information as the writer; include all available information pertinent to the issues being discussed, so everyone reading the plan will have the same frame of reference.

CONDUCTING RESEARCH

In preparing your business review, data can be obtained through both primary and secondary research. If you employ a research firm, an advertising agency that conducts research, or an in-house research department, primary research is the most effective way of obtaining data specific to your market, your product, and your competitors. If you do not have access to a professional researcher, however, we recommend that you do not try to do primary research yourself but rely on secondary research—data compiled by outside sources.

The business review examples presented in Chapter 2 rely heavily on secondary research and your own company sales and marketing data to provide you with a marketing information base. However, we strongly recommend that if possible, both secondary and primary research be utilized in preparing a marketing database and business review. If you don't have a research program in place, you might develop the framework for a research program in your current plan so that the information will be available for the following year's planning process.

Primary Research

Original research compiled to meet your specific data requirements is broken down into two categories, quantitative and qualitative.

Quantitative Research

The data and information are usually obtained through surveys, with data gathered from a representative random sample of a given universe. The samples are large enough to make inferences that are statistically significant. We refer to two types of quantitative research methods most often throughout this book. One is customer based research, which provides information about a company's own customers. The other is marketwide research, which is used to provide information about the overall category user/purchaser base.

Qualitative Research

Research methods, such as focus groups, that do not statistically represent the target market universe provide qualitative data. Qualitative research typically involves small groups of consumers who are asked to provide insights into their likes and dislikes of a particular product and why and how they purchase or use one type of product versus another. Qualitative research is also used to gain insights into the strengths and weaknesses of advertising and other forms of communication.

Qualitative research is used to add depth and richness to quantitative findings. For example, quantitative research may determine that a company has a perceived customer service problem relative to the competition. Qualitative research can be used to help further explain what consumers feel customer service entails in the company's particular industry and what specifically is lacking in the company's customer service compared to other companies.

Qualitative research can also be very useful in determining the key issues to include in a quantitative research study. Particularly if there has been no previous research, a company may want to utilize a focus group to provide added insights into consumer thinking prior to formulating a quantitative study. The information and insights gained from initial qualitative research can then be verified through quantitative, statistical research.

Finally, a word of caution. Used by itself, qualitative research can be very misleading. It is not statistically based; a roomful of 10 people is often a poor representation of what the marketplace really thinks. Qualitative research is most valuable when used as an enriching tool to quantitatively defined observations.

Secondary Research

Secondary research, which may also be quantitative or qualitative, is not specifically compiled for your company but rather is existing information and is available through outside sources. An example of a secondary research source is census information. Combining this type of secondary research information with your company's data will allow you to develop insights into your customers, your market, and the problems and opportunities facing your company, just as is done with primary research. The only difference is that primary research is conducted to answer specific questions. To answer these questions with secondary research, you may have to dig a little more and be willing to analyze multiple studies instead of just one to find your answers. And even then, sometimes you may not be able to answer all your questions and will have to rely on judgment.

INDEXING

Indexing is used extensively in the business review and is a process that presents a number or group of numbers in relation to a specific number—an average, or base. It is a method of showing a relationship between two sets of numbers or percentages. Indexing is based on using 100 as the average. Anything over 100 means the index is greater than the average; anything below 100 is less than the average.

When indexing, a base number is established and all other numbers are compared to it. For example, assume 60 percent of the population owns a home, and home ownership is further broken down by age category as shown in Exhibit 1.1. Since 60 percent is the average percentage of home ownership, it becomes the base number from which to measure any subset of the population. For example, among 18 to 24 year olds, only 20 percent own homes, so 20 percent divided by 60 percent equals .33. For purposes of clarity and easier communications, the decimal is then multiplied by 100 to give a round number (.33 x 100 equals an index of 33). From this point on in the book, we will not explicitly show the multiplication by 100. Thirty-three is substantially below 100; thus 18 to 24 year olds own homes at one-third the average across all ages.

In another example, 30 percent of a national company's consumers live in Chicago, so you'd expect them to consume 30 percent of the product (30 divided by 30 = an index of 100, or average). But if Chicago consumers consume 60 percent of the company's product, they are consuming at a rate of 60 percent, divided by the base of 30 percent, for an index of 200. Thus, the Chicago market would compare at twice the national average, or 100 points above the expected consumption pattern.

When using indexing, we usually consider an index meaningful if it is plus or minus 10 from 100. In other words, we look for numbers 110 and above

EXHIBIT 1.1 Indexing Example

Age Category	Home Ownership*	Index
18 to 24	20%	33
25 to 34	48	80
35 to 44	60	100
45 to 54	74	123
55 to 64	70	117
65 to 74	50	83
Average—all ages	60	100

*These numbers are used only for example. They do not reflect current home ownership rates.

or 90 and below. If all age groups index between 95 and 105 in terms of consumption, we determine that our target market is flat across all age groups. However, if the 25 to 34 and 35 to 44 age groups indexed at 115 and 180, respectively, and all other age groups were at or below average (or below 100), then we would determine that those two age groups consumed at significantly higher levels.

How to Prepare
a Business Review

The business review is organized into ten steps. Within each step are questions to be addressed that ensure the information collection activity is properly focused. Some of the questions have corresponding charts. These charts are designed to assist you in efficiently organizing the data so that the answers can be easily derived. Some of the sections may not directly apply to your business, but we suggest you follow each, paying particular attention to those that are most relevant to your type of business.

The key to developing a 1-day marketing plan is to prepare the business review during the weeks prior to actually writing the plan. If this is not possible, answer the questions most pertinent to your business situation. Use the "directional" information principle discussed in Chapter 1, making best estimates based on your knowledge and others' knowledge of the industry. Remember, this information base will form the foundation for decisions made when developing the marketing plan.

OVERVIEW

Now that you have an understanding of what is involved in a business review, you are ready to read through each step of the review. Each contains two main components.

- *Marketing questions* that must be answered in order to provide an adequate quantitative database for each section.

- *Charts* to help you organize your information in a disciplined manner, so you will be able to answer the marketing questions accurately. The charts are examples of a format you can easily adapt to your own situation. Worksheets for each of these charts are provided at the end of this chapter.

The charts are intended to help you organize your data search. They are not exhaustive and cover only the major topical areas. Therefore, it is not intended that all the questions at the end of each business review section will have a corresponding chart. Many of the charts provide multiple pieces of information when completed. For example, one of the sales charts provides sales trends for the industry and for your company, demonstrates differences in industry growth compared to your company's growth, and provides company market share data.

While the charts are used primarily to assure that your information is organized to allow you to answer the questions following each business review section, they can also be used as support for business review conclusions during presentations. In addition, you may want to consider transferring the information in the charts onto graphs for presentation purposes. Graphs provide a better visual interpretation than charts, which tend to get very busy with numbers. Finally, please note that two of the ten steps (1, Corporate Philosophy; and 5, Awareness and Product Attributes) do not require further detail and charts.

DEVELOPING THE BUSINESS REVIEW

In developing your own business review, it is important to realize that you may not have the resources or time to complete all portions. There will be portions that do not pertain to your business. Remember that this chapter covers information important to business-to-business firms, consumer goods firms (firms that manufacture consumer goods and sell to retailers, who in turn sell to the ultimate consumer), retailers, and service businesses. While most marketing questions apply to all business categories, there are some that are clearly applicable to only one or another of these business categories. This should be evident to you as you go through the chapter.

Step 1: Corporate Philosophy/Description of the Company and Products

Different companies are unique in the ways they do business, their historical backgrounds, and their organizational structures, all of which have some level of impact on the development of a marketing plan. It is important to briefly describe, up front, predetermined corporate objectives, pertinent company and product history, and current product information and organizational parameters. By considering the culture and aspirations of the organization before writing the marketing plan, you stand a better chance of developing a plan that will be effectively implemented throughout the organization.

Corporate Goals and Objectives: Questions

- What are the long-term and short-term goals, mission, and objectives of the company? Are there existing sales goals, profit goals, or marketing objectives?

- What is the operating budget for the company? What are the margins and what are the planned profit contributions of each product?
- Is there a corporate philosophy on how to do business? What are the principles of the business in regard to working with customers, developing and selling product, and internal management?

General Company and Product History: Questions

- What is the history of your company? Why was it started, how did it grow, and why is it successful?

- What products does your company sell? What is the makeup of your products? What advantages do your products have over the competition?

- What is the history of your products? Have they always been as successful? Why were they first marketed? Over the years, how have your products changed?

- What is the sales volume, margin, and profitability of each product or product line (five-year trend)? What product categories are most important to the company?

- Do the products your company manufactures or sells have any potential manufacturing problems? Are specialized parts, labor, or manufacturing processes necessary? Are the products vulnerable to shortages or other consumer, environmental, or economic factors? If so, how?

- What plans are there for growth and expansion among *existing product categories?* New products? More markets geographically? New product uses? Market share development within current categories?

- Are there plans for growth and expansion among *new product categories?* Do you plan to go into any new additional categories?

- What single thing does your company want to be known for? What are you best at? Why do consumers purchase from you?

- How has your product category done nationally? What are the trends over the past five years in terms of product innovation, marketing, distribution, pricing, and merchandising? What is expected for the future?

- Where has your company succeeded and failed? Why?

Company Organization: Questions

- How is your company organized from top to bottom? What does your organization chart look like?

- Is your marketing department sufficiently organized to develop and execute a disciplined marketing plan? Do you have enough resources to plan, implement, and analyze results?

- To what degree is the company committed to marketing? Where does marketing fit in your overall organizational structure?

- Does your marketing department have the ability to communicate with and have a positive impact on other departments within the company?

- Does your marketing department have influence over all the marketing tools and the decisions made regarding sales, product, pricing, distribution, advertising, media, promotion, publicity, and merchandising?

- Is the company operations driven, finance driven, merchandise driven, product driven, sales driven, or marketing driven? In other words, what area of the company is most responsible for the company's success? Will that be true in the future? How does the marketing department fit in? How will this affect your ability to develop and implement effective marketing plans?

Step 2: Review of the Consumer Target Market

Target market definition is the most important phase in preparing a business review. Effective marketing is impossible without a thorough understanding of your *current* and *potential* customer base. The better the customer is understood, the better the marketer is able to fulfill the customer's needs.

The business review provides a format that sorts current and potential customers into segments. Segmenting allows customers to be grouped according to common demographic, product usage, and purchasing characteristics. This allows for the analysis of which customer group is currently most profitable and which consumer group has the most potential for your company. The end result of segmenting is that a company is able to focus its marketing resources against an ultimate target market that has common demographic and product usage characteristics, purchasing habits, and product or service needs. Instead of trying to be all things to all people, the company can direct its energies toward satisfying essentially one person as characterized by the target market segment or segments.

The business review further provides a format that describes the profile of the current *category consumer* as compared to the *company's current customer*. This allows the marketer to determine if the company's customer is different from the general product category consumer. The similarities and differences will be important when determining future marketing strategies. A company may find that its product is consumed by a far older population than the general product category's consumer. This important information can be used in the marketing plan to further target this older age segment or to develop plans to attract more of the younger, mainstream consumer.

Demographics and Lifestyle Factors

The marketer's traditional method of defining purchaser and user groups and segmenting markets is by utilizing demographic factors. Demographics can be determined for either individuals or households (the configuration of individuals making up a living unit). Marketers also use lifestyle factors or psychographics to help develop target markets. Lifestyle descriptors help to define a customer segment in terms of the attitudes, interests, and activities of the consumer.

Questions

- What is the consumer demographic profile of the product category nationally? What is the profile of the individuals who consume or purchase the most from a volume standpoint?

- What is the percentage of population that uses the product? Are you marketing a mass market product or a specialty market product?

- What is your customer's demographic profile? How would you describe your customers in terms of age, sex, income, occupation, education, number of children, marital status, geographic residence, and ownership of home?

- What are your customers' attitudes, interests, and activities? How would you describe them from a lifestyle standpoint?

- Are your customers different in terms of demographic and lifestyle characteristics from the overall category consumer profile?

- How many consumers purchase your product? How many potential consumers exist? Has the number of consumers been growing or shrinking over the past five years?

- Do religious, political, or other socioeconomic factors make a difference in the purchase of your product or service?

Product Usage

For some products, demographics aren't as important as why the product is purchased or how it is used. Many times purchasers with similar demographics purchase the product for different reasons. This offers the opportunity to segment consumers based on usage of the product. Baking soda is purchased by people who bake from scratch; it is also purchased as a refrigerator deodorizer. Many of the purchasers of baking soda as a deodorizer do not bake on a regular basis and so do not purchase the product for baking. Thus, usage of this product helps define customer segments, and knowledge of the customers' usage is critical for how this product would be marketed to each of the two customer groups.

Questions

- How is your product used? Are there multiple uses?

- Why is your product purchased? What are the benefits inherent in your product that encourage consumers to purchase?

- If there are multiple uses of your product, are there consumers who use the product for one type of use or benefit but not another? Are there multiple, independent user groups?

- Do the different user groups have differing demographics? What is their size in terms of volume or purchases and number of consumers?

Heavy Users

Most product categories have a group of heavy users—consumers who purchase or use the product at far greater rates than that of the average consumer. According to our definition, a category has a meaningful heavy users segment if approximately *one-third or less of the consumers account for approximately two-thirds or more of the purchases.* A retail example of this can be found in the shoe business. One-third of the purchasers buy more than 63 percent of the shoes. The demographic description of the heavy user shoe purchaser is women age 25 to 44 with children. A heavy user shoe purchaser is further defined as someone who purchases seven or more pairs of shoes per year. (The average person purchases fewer than three pairs per year.)

Heavy users are important because they offer the potential of marketing to a smaller, more defined group of people who account for the majority of purchases. If you do not have primary research that determines the percentage of purchases attributable to the heavy user, you can make direction estimates by using Simmons Market Research Bureau (SMRB) or other secondary sources. If nothing is available to you, make the best estimate based on your knowledge of the market.

In summary, it is important to determine if there is a heavy user group in your product category. Then develop a demographic profile of the heavy user group to determine if it is similar to your customer profile.

Questions

- Is there a group of heavy purchasers of your product? What percentage of the purchasers do they constitute, and what percentage of the purchases are they responsible for?

- What is the difference in the demographic and lifestyle profile of the heavy user and that of the overall user?

- Is the heavy user profile similar to that of your customer profile?

Potential Primary and Secondary Target Markets

Primary Target Market. A primary target market is your main consuming group. This group of consumers are the most important purchasers and users of your product and will be the mainstay of your business. In some cases, it is the heavy user. For other companies who are more specialist oriented, it will be a smaller though viable section of the market that requires unique goods and services.

Many times the purchaser of a product is different from the user. If this is true, you need to decide who has most influence over the actual purchase. If the wife does the grocery shopping, does the husband who drinks the beer request his brand preference, or does he drink what his wife buys him? In most cases, the individual who does the purchasing becomes the primary target market. However, when the purchaser primarily buys what the user requests, then the user receives primary attention.

The primary target market becomes the company's reason for being. You are in business to determine the primary target market's wants and needs and to provide for those wants and needs better than your competition. This pertains to providing the product, service, shopping environment, distribution channel, and price structure that is required by the customer for purchase. The better the definition and description of the consumers in your primary target market, the better you will be able to market to them.

Secondary Target Markets. Secondary target markets are important because they provide additional sales to the company beyond that of the primary target market, as well as future sales to the company. This group of people can also help to influence the usage rate and purchases of the primary target market. A secondary target market can be one of the following:

- *Influencers.* Influencers can be either a primary or secondary target market, though in most situations they are a secondary target market. These are individuals who influence the purchase or usage decision of the primary target market. A good example of this is the influence children have on their parents in the purchase of many consumer goods, from toys to fast food meals.

- *A demographic category with a high concentration index.* Often there is a distinct demographic category that accounts for a small percentage of the volume but contains a high concentration of purchasers. For example, 18 to 24 year olds may account for only 10 percent of the total product category purchases, but 50 percent of the 18 to 24 year olds may purchase the product. This could happen for two reasons: (1) the small size of the target market relative to other target markets, or (2) smaller purchasing rates or purchases of more inexpensive product models.

- *Subsets of purchasers or users who make up the primary target markets.* As stated in the primary target market section, ideally your primary target market should be one unified profile of customers. This allows for a focusing of resources and message in the marketing effort. However, there are situations where the volume of any one target market is not substantial enough to qualify it as a primary target market. In this case, the marketer is forced to develop a broader primary market profile to meet the primary target market criteria of accounting for approximately 50 percent of the product category volume. In doing this, the primary target profile encompasses many unique subsets of users who have slightly different demographics, needs, wants, product usage, and purchasing behavior. These subsets should be delineated in greater detail in the secondary target market section.

Questions

- Are there several distinct types of consumer descriptions? What is the size of each target market? Do you have multiple consumer profiles or one main one?

- Are users of the product also the purchasers? If not, who has the most influence over the purchaser's decision?

- When the product is purchased, are there individuals who, although they do not make the actual purchase, have a substantial influence on the purchaser? To what extent? How would you describe these?

- Does your primary target market account for approximately 50 percent of the sales volume, or are you going to specialize against a very narrow segment? If so, can this segment support your company? Is it large enough, based on sales volume projections of the segment and market share projections for your company? (See Step 10, Demand Analysis, for further detail.)

- Can you define one narrow and focused profile of your target customer? What is it?

- Is the primary target market growing, stable, or shrinking?

- Are there distinct secondary target markets for your product that have common characteristics apart from the primary target market?

Step 3: Review of the Business-to-Business Target Market

Business-to-business firms typically have far fewer potential customers than do consumer companies. In addition, each business-to-business customer usually generates larger sales than does the typical consumer customer. As with consumer target markets, it is important to segment so you can determine which type of business is most profitable and has the most potential for your company.

Target Market Segmentation and Standard Industrial Classification (SIC) Categories

One of the best ways to segment businesses is by utilizing Standard Industrial Classification (SIC) codes. Or, use the same SIC methodology to segment by other functional classifications that pertain to your particular product category. Businesses are classified into ten different broad, two-digit SIC categories: Agriculture/Forestry/Fishing, Mining, Manufacturing, Construction, Transportation/Communication/Public Utilities, Whole-sale Trade, Retail Trade, Finance/Insurance/Real Estate, Services, and Public Administration. Within each two-digit SIC category, there are further breakouts into four- and eight-digit classifications. Within the Retail SIC there is category 56, Apparel and Accessory Stores, and within category 56 there is 5611, Men's and Boy's Clothing.

Firms such as Dun's Marketing Services specialize in providing mailing lists and other market information for businesses according to any SIC classification. We have used Dun's to target specific types of business by industry type. We helped generate incremental sales for a statewide CPA firm by creating individual campaigns for small businesses within each SIC code. Different tailored messages were developed for retailers, the service industry, financial institutions, etc. Each industry received multiple marketing pieces explaining why specialized accounting practices were important for their specific business. The campaign was so successful that for every $1 the CPA firm invested, it had a return of $2—a 100 percent return on investment over a two-year period.

Base Segmenting

The first step in developing business-to-business target market segments is to break down your customer base by purchaser segment or SIC. Next, determine how many different business categories you sell to. List the categories in which you have the most customers or clients first, and then continue listing the categories in sequential order from most customers to least. Finally, determine the penetration of each category (percentage of the total category that you can classify as a customer).

You may be surprised that you are doing business with multiple categories of businesses. You may also find that there are some categories that can provide a large degree of growth potential, categories where you do business with only a small percentage of the total. This information will help you define target markets and develop marketing strategies later in the plan.

Questions

- To what SIC categories do customers who purchase your product belong?
- In what categories are you doing the most business? In what categories are you doing the least business?
- What is the demand potential for your product? What is the penetration of your company in each SIC category? How many businesses are there in SIC categories that purchase product in your category but are not purchasing from you? Why aren't they?

Other Methods of Segmenting

Once you have your target market broken into SIC categories, there are additional criteria you should evaluate to further allow for a complete understanding of your target market.

Dollar Size. Determine the total company sales volume for each SIC. Then calculate the average dollar size of each client in the categories by dividing the total company volume in each SIC by the number of clients you have in that SIC. This can tell you a lot about current and future potential of the different categories when combined with the penetration information developed earlier. If an SIC classification averages substantially above other SIC classifications in terms of average dollar per client, and your company has not fully penetrated the classification (your company's clients represent a small percentage of the total businesses in the SIC), then that classification should be targeted for further expansion.

Number of Employees. Another way to segment business is by the number of employees or employee size of the firm. Employee size often is an indicator of the company's volume *and* how they do business. For example, large companies tend to be more centralized with formalized organizational structures, while smaller companies tend to be less formalized. Pricing, product, and service requirements often differ between large and small companies. Thus, the marketing approach may differ as a function of the size of the business customer.

Heavy Usage Rates. Are there heavy or light user categories? Determine the reasons why. Maybe a category of light users would become heavier users if you were to modify your product, service, or pricing. Or perhaps you should consider narrowing your firm's focus to concentrate on just the heavy user categories, especially if the earlier analysis determined that there was potential growth in these categories.

Product Application/Use. Essentially this is how the organization uses your product. If you find that there are several different uses for your product, you can segment target markets by usage type and begin to provide more focused service and expertise to each segment.

Organizational Structure. Different companies have different organizational structures. Find out if your company sells better to one type of company than another. You might find you get more business from centralized organizations with formalized bidding procedures and thus want to target these types of businesses within the SICs you currently service. Or you might analyze why you don't do as well with decentralized entrepreneurial firms and make changes to increase your success with them. Subsequently, you may do well targeting headquarters but perform poorly in generating sales from branches. In summary, you may need to develop independent marketing strategies and executions for different target groups as defined by their organizational structure, purchasing habits, and purchasing requirements.

New versus Repeat Buyer. Some companies are good at getting new business and weak at developing long-term relationships. For others it's just the opposite. Determine the percentage of your business that comes from new buyers versus repeat buyers. Correct your weaknesses if it becomes evident that you either aren't getting new business or can't develop long-term clients. This area is a good client satisfaction check and should be analyzed yearly. It also allows you to develop alternative marketing strategies depending on the type of customer (new versus repeat) you are targeting.

Geographic Location. In analyzing sales, you may determine that you are strong in one part of the country but weak in another. It could be because of your distribution system. It might be a competitive situation, or you may find that demand is higher in some geographical areas than others. In addition, you might discover that you do very well against a particular SIC category in one region of the country but haven't marketed to that SIC category elsewhere. By analyzing where your current business exists and where you have potential to expand, you can segment your target market by geographic location.

Decision Makers and Influencers. Finally, you need to determine who actually decides to purchase your product and who influences the purchase of your product. Analyze the purchase decision making process. Describe who makes the ultimate purchasing decision, how they arrive at the purchasing decision, what the purchasing criteria are, and to what degree people influence the purchaser. The purchaser may in fact be a committee, which means you will need to target many individuals if all have an equal role in the decision process. Typically, the decision maker or purchaser becomes your primary target market, and those individuals influencing the decision become the secondary target market.

Questions

- What is the total company sales volume by SIC, and what is the average sales volume per customer?

- What is the revenue distribution of your customers by SIC? Does it correlate to the number of clients in each SIC, or do some categories have a higher average dollar per client figure?

- What size are the companies that purchase from you? Do large companies respond differently from small ones? If so, why?

- Are there heavy users *within* SIC categories? Are some SIC categories heavier users than others?

- Do different SIC category businesses use your product for different purposes? Why do SIC categories need/use your product? Is your product used more by some industries than by others? Can you expand use to others?

- Are purchasers of your product original equipment manufacturers (OEMs) who utilize your product in the manufacturing of another product? And do they sell to another business or directly to the consumer? How exactly does your product fit into the OEM's manufacturing structure? Why is your product important? How is it used?

- What is the organizational structure of your customers' companies? Do you have more success with centralized companies than with decentralized? Why? Do purchasing procedures differ among customers? Do you get more business from companies with a single purchasing agent versus a purchasing committee that requires more formalized bidding?

- Are the majority of your customers new or repeat buyers? Why?

- Where are your customers located? Are there areas of the country that have businesses from SIC categories that you are successful with but that you currently are not covering? Are there potential customers that match your customer profile but that you are not reaching? Do some parts of the country provide more business for you than others? If so, why? Is it due to servicing, distribution, sales efforts, or competitive factors? Or do some parts of the country use more product than other parts for other reasons?

- Who are the decision makers and influencers in the purchase of your product? What is the decision maker's function and role in the purchase decision? What is the decision sequence and purchase criteria?

Step 4: Sales Analysis

Sales data can be analyzed many different ways. Properly analyzed, the data can provide the marketer with a wealth of information. The key, however, is to break down total sales into actionable segments of information to gain a clear understanding of what is taking place within your company as compared to the industry or product category as a whole. Wherever possible use five-year trend data.

Total Sales

- Is the overall product category strong? Is it growing or declining? What are industry sales for the past five years? What is the percentage increase over that period?

- What are the total company sales and profit levels for the past five years? What is the growth rate? What is the growth rate compared to the industry and compared to your key competitors?

- Are market sales likely to expand or shrink in the next two, five, or ten years? How will this affect your company?

Sales by Brand or Department

- Now that you have charted your company's total sales, what are the sales and profit trends for your individual products, services, or departments over the past five years? What is the growth rate relative to the national average or key competitors' products, services, or departments? Why?

- What products, services, or departments show the most potential in relationship to sales and profit within your *company?* What products, services, or departments show the most potential in terms of sales and profit relative to the *national category* and *competitive products?*

- Which products are above or below the budgeted margin over the past five years? Which products have the highest margin and the lowest margin?

Market Share

- What is the market share of your total company sales within your industry over the past five years? Are you gaining or losing market share? Why?

- What is the market share for each of your company's products or departments relative to the national product category or relative to key competitors' products or departments market share over the past five years? Are you gaining or losing market share? Why?

- What competitors have gained/lost the most market share? Why?

Store-for-Store for Retailers

- What are store-for-store sales over the past five years? Have they been increasing or decreasing? How do they compare to total sales?

- Is there a certain per store sales average that must be met to break even?

- Which markets are above the break even point and which are below?

- Which stores/markets are above or below budgeted sales and profits?

Seasonality of Sales

- What is the total sales seasonality for your business?

- What *products* sell during what times of the year? Does demand vary by season, business conditions, location, or weather?

- How do your company sales differ from the total category's sales? Is there a time of the year in which you don't do as well or in which you outperform the industry as a whole? What is the seasonality of your company's product and the product category as a whole?

- Do specific products have strong seasonal selling periods that differ from the category nationally?

- For retailers, what are the weekly and daily seasonality trends of your product? Which days of the week are strong in sales relative to others? Which weeks are strong in sales relative to others?

Sales by Geographic Territory/Target Market Segments

- Are there areas of the country that provide more total sales and profits and/or sales per capita than others? Why?

- Are there target market segments that account for more total sales and profits or sales per capita than others? Why?

Step 5: Product Awareness and Product Attributes

We have documented in case after case that an increase in awareness of a quality product leads to increases in purchase rates or, in the terminology of our agency, *increased share of mind leads to increased share of purchases*. Therefore, awareness of your product or service is an important barometer of its future success.

Product Awareness

Typically, awareness is measured through primary research on two levels, unaided and aided. *Unaided* awareness is generally considered a more accurate measure. It involves consumers recalling specific product names without any assistance. *Aided* awareness is the awareness generated by asking individuals which product they are familiar with after reading or reviewing with them a list of competing products.

Awareness measures allow the marketing manager to fine tune advertising message and media strategies. Some examples of how awareness is used to help formulate subsequent marketing strategies are the following:

- Low awareness levels signal the need for a more aggressive or effective advertising and promotional plan. Often, the primary problem is that the product has low awareness among consumers, not that the product necessarily needs a repositioning. This is especially true if the product has positive attribute ratings from current users and a high trial/repeat usage ratio.

- Markets with high levels of awareness often don't need as much media weight to sustain existing sales levels as markets with low awareness. And it often requires less media weight to generate successful promotions in established markets with high awareness than in newer markets where a customer base is not yet established and a minimal number of potential consumers have heard of your product or company. As an example, markets in which a product has low awareness often require larger print ads than markets with higher awareness levels. Our experience has shown that small newspaper ads are more likely to be seen by current users, and it takes larger ads to attract the attention of infrequent users or individuals who are not aware of your product.

- Markets with falling awareness levels often indicate isolated market specific problems such as increased competitive activity. These problems may require an individual marketing plan tailored to the specific market situation along with investment spending over the short term to stabilize and increase awareness levels.

If you cannot afford primary research, we would encourage you to informally conduct an awareness study for your product. Randomly call individuals or companies in your geographic selling area. Ask them if they have used products in your category in the past year. If they have, ask them to name all the stores in the area where they can purchase the product category (for retailers), or to name all the brands they are familiar with in the product category. This will provide insight to unaided awareness, the purest awareness measure. Try to get between 100 and 200 responses. Also keep track of *first mentions* (those products/stores mentioned first by each respondent without receiving assistance); this is a good prediction of your company's market share relative to the competition.

With this information you can infer what percentage of the potential customer base is aware of your product and where it ranks relative to the competition. This will provide a rough approximation of unaided awareness levels for your product and that of the competition. You can also determine the first mention level, a strong indication of market share, actual use of the product, or propensity to use, since customers will most often mention first a brand or company name they normally use the most.

Questions

- What is the unaided and aided awareness of your product compared to the competition? Have awareness levels been increasing or decreasing over the past five years?

- What is the first mention level (first product mentioned) by consumers without receiving assistance?

Product Attributes

Product attributes or benefits are derived from consumers' perceptions of the product. This step of the business review is critical to developing future marketing plans, for it allows the marketing manager to define the strengths and weaknesses of the company's product relative to the competition. It is necessary to find what attributes are important to purchasers and users of your product and then determine how your company or product compares to the competition on these attributes. There may be attributes that you need to improve. Or you may find there are certain needs that no one in the marketplace is fulfilling, providing your company the opportunity to dominate an important niche. The repositioning of a menswear chain we worked with was brought about because the retailer determined that the most important attributes to the target market were quality and value, not low purchase price, which was being emphasized. The repositioning emphasized value (a good price on perceived quality brands). The theme line became "Ross and Ross for Businessmenswear," which denoted a special quality and expertise and labeled a specific group of people identified with quality men's clothing.

Questions

The information to answer these questions is normally obtained through primary research. If your company cannot afford to undertake primary research to answer these questions, then you should use available secondary research and attempt to answer them yourself in as much detail as possible. Also, have other individuals in your organization answer them to see if your perceptions match those of your co-workers. Perhaps even get other individuals outside of your company to answer the questions to compare with answers from people within your organization.

- How is your product used? What is the product's primary benefit to the consumer?

- What are the important product attributes of your product's category? What are the important attributes of your competitors' products? How do your company's products rank on those attributes versus the competition?

- What do purchasers and users like and dislike about your product?

- Are there differences between heavy users' likes and dislikes compared to the overall user of your product category?

- Are there substitutes that can be used in place of your company's product or the product category?

- Is there anything unusual about how your product is manufactured or designed that would be of interest or benefit to consumers? Is there anything about your product that can help differentiate it from the competition? For example, how is it manufactured? Does it have a unique color, shape, or texture? Does your product last longer than others like it? What about guarantees? Are there unique performance attributes that make it superior to the competition? Is there unique packaging? Is your product more convenient to use than the competitor's? Is your product of better quality? What about the competitors' products?

- Are there any inherent product qualities that have not been communicated but are important to the buyer? (Same for your competition.)

- If you have many competitors, how does your product rank in terms of overall quality? How does your product rank in terms of value (the combination of quality and price)? Where does your product rank in terms of performance, durability, serviceability, and aesthetic appearance compared to the competition?

- What is the history of your product? When was it first marketed? What changes have been made to the product and why? (Same for your competition.)

- Is your product accepted by a broad consumer base or a narrow segment? Why?

- Does your product have any patents that are active? Does your unique advantage depend on a specific design, formula, or manufacturing capability that could be readily copied? Or is your product unique due to patent protection or some manufacturing process that is difficult or costly to duplicate?

- What are the new developments in your product category? What will be the next big innovation? What product improvements are consumers looking for?

Step 6: Purchase Rates/Buying Habits

The marketer should analyze purchase rates and buying habits to further determine where, how, and why consumers are purchasing the company's product. Buying habit information can provide invaluable insight into the target market and provide impact for marketing decisions during the writing of the marketing plan. These decisions revolve around either trying to change current consumption patterns (which is more difficult) or recognizing the patterns and modifying the product or the way the product is sold to better meet the needs of the target market.

Purchase Rates of the Product Category and Your Company's Product by Geographic Markets

Geographic markets should be analyzed for their importance in sales for the category and sales for your company's product. Look for markets where the product category does very well from a sales per capita standpoint, but your company's product is either not marketed or is not doing well relative to other markets. If the category is performing well in these markets, there exists potential you may want to tap in the subsequent marketing plan. In addition, it is helpful to identify strong company markets so that you can protect them and keep them strong. Finally, you need to identify the weaker company markets and develop alternative plans to grow them or decide that you will fund only the profitable markets. Before these decisions are made, you need a clear picture of the strength of your markets on a geographic basis.

Questions

- Where exactly do your customers reside? Are they distributed nationwide or are they limited to certain regions? Are they living in large cities, suburbs, or rural areas (C and D counties)?

- Where are sales for your *product category* strongest and weakest nationally? Where are your *company's sales* strongest and weakest?

- What markets have above or below average purchase rates for your product on a household or per person basis? Does your company have different geographical distribution from that of the category in general?

- Are national sales increasing at greater or lesser rates than the population growth? Are there specific markets where this is different?

Trading Areas

In addition to geographic information, the retail/service marketer should determine the trading area for the product. A trading area is the geographical territory where your customers live. This is important not only from a media purchasing standpoint but also for determining future store locations, as discussed in Chapter 10, Distribution.

Questions

- What is the trading area for your product? How far do consumers travel to purchase your product?

Brand Loyalty

Brand loyalty is a measure of how loyal your customers are over a period of time. If your customers primarily use only your company's product, they are brand loyal. If they use your product most of the time but occasionally use your competitors' products, they are moderately brand loyal. And if brand or product switching occurs regularly, there exists low brand loyalty.

Brand loyalty is analyzed to provide insights into the following types of issues:

- How difficult it will be to keep your own customers.

- How difficult it will be to steal market share from competitors.

- The degree of promotional offers that will be needed to induce trial.

- How much media weight will be necessary to increase trial, retrial, and sales.

- Whether a true product difference or innovation is needed to compete.

Obviously, a product category with extremely high brand loyalty will require more media weight, larger promotional offers or inducements, and perhaps even a product innovation to be able to steal market share from existing competitors. With a low brand loyalty type of product category, it is extremely difficult to keep your own customers, but it is also easier to steal market share.

Questions

- Is buying by brand name important to consumers in your category? What percentage of the consumers in the category are brand loyal most of the time, all of the time, or never?

- How brand loyal are your customers? Is brand switching common? Do heavy users have different loyalty than the overall users?

Buying Habits

Buying habits, such as frequency of purchase, also need to be determined. In analyzing the average time between purchases, the marketer can make decisions about how frequently the business needs to advertise and promote the product. This information also helps when making promotion decisions. If the product is purchased only once a year, a viable strategy would be to provide a strong incentive for purchase prior to the typical purchasing season. Or, if the purchase decision is made frequently at short intervals, a continuity program of lower media weight levels might be required.

In addition to frequency of purchase, the marketer should also determine whether the purchase decision is made spontaneously in-store or planned prior to shopping. We did work for a product that was purchased spontaneously in-store 90 percent of the time. Obviously, point-of-purchase advertising and display became critical to the product's success.

Finally, in looking at buying habits, everything about the purchasing environment should be analyzed: the psychology of the purchaser at the time of the purchase, the average purchase ratio (for retailers, this is the number of times a consumer comes into a retail store and purchases, versus not purchasing and walking), and the actual purchasing habits. This information will lead to strategic marketing decisions aimed at better meeting the needs of the target market.

Questions

- What factors are important to the purchase decision making process? What is the purchase decision sequence a consumer makes when purchasing your product? How can you positively affect this?

- How frequently are purchases made? What is the purchase cycle for your product or service? What is the frequency of purchase for all users versus heavy users?

- What is the size and quantity of each purchase? (One, two, three bars of soap per trip; large, medium, or small package sizes?) Do consumers purchase in bulk, stock up, or do consumers purchase your product one at a time?

- What is the purchase ratio? What percentage of customers purchases when they visit the store?

- What percentage of the product category purchases are on sale or at discount? What percentage of your company product purchases are on sale or discounted? What is the average sale or discount percentage? Are there times of the year when sales or discounting occur at greater rates than others?

- How important is customer service, personal selling, salesperson advice/consultation to the purchaser or the purchase decision?

- Is the buying decision spontaneous (made in-store) or planned? What percentage of buying decisions are made at the point of purchase versus at home or over a longer period of time?

- Do the heavy users have different buying habits than the overall users?

Trial and Retrial

Another important area of investigation is trial and retrial. The Hiebing Group did work for a dominant national client that had a specialty line of consumer package goods products. The product sold was basically the same, but each was packaged for specific uses—packages for the car, the teenager's bedroom, dad's work area, and the woman's purse. The initial thinking was that we would expand usage categories for the products, in other words, find other places besides the car for consumers to use that product. However, after studying the buying habit findings in the situation analysis, we discovered two things: (1) overall trial of the family of products was very low, and (2) of those people who tried the products, retrial was very high.

In summary, the challenge was not in finding more uses for the family of products, but in promoting trial. Once consumers tried one of the products, the chances were good they would continue to purchase them. However, if we had found that the retrial rate was in fact very poor, we would have had another set of *product-related* problems to focus on, thus taking our marketing emphasis in the direction of finding out why customers weren't satisfied with the product and how to better satisfy them.

Questions

- What percentage of the customer base has tried your product?

- How common is retrial? What percentage becomes regular users?

- Do heavy users have different trial and retrial rates than the overall users?

Step 7: Distribution

Distribution is the method of delivering the product to the consumer. In the business review, your job is to determine which method of distribution is used most successfully by the industry, your company, and your competitors. However, the concept of distribution varies depending on the type of business category.

Retail

Retailers need to be aware of how and where their product is sold in relation to the industry. There are many unique ways to distribute the product to the consumer, and retailers should be aware of which distribution methods are increasing or decreasing in their industry and the advantages and disadvantages of the different methods.

Channel Type/Trends. The retailer has to determine and review the optimum outlet category for the product being sold and the consumer who is purchasing. Common retail distribution outlet categories include mass merchandise, discount, off-price, department stores, specialty shops, chain stores, and direct mail. Each is a unique distribution method a retailer can use to sell the product to the consumer. To do this, it helps to analyze the current channel trends. The business review may determine that for your product category, the two fastest growing methods of distribution are smaller, single-line specialty shops and direct mail. If you were not currently using these channels, you would need to address the industry's shift in emphasis toward these alternative methods of distribution in the marketing plan. This could be done by adapting some of the strengths of specialty store retailing to your channel environment or by experimenting with direct mail.

Geography. The geographical distribution of outlets should be studied. Try to grade the location of your stores relative to your competitors. Is your firm located in the optimal trading areas of the market? Are they easy to get to and do they have good access? Are they on or near thoroughfares with high traffic counts and other thriving retail locations? Are there markets or specific trading areas within markets that have large numbers of purchases per person and/or household and low levels of competition where you should be doing business?

Penetration. Optimum penetration levels (number of stores per market) should be calculated to determine whether more distribution outlets are needed. Note that in the broadest sense we define *markets* as DMAs—Designated Market Areas or Television Coverage Areas—but markets can be defined in terms of a DMA, SMSA (Standard Metropolitan Statistical Area), county, or city/metro trading area. Penetration levels are evaluated on three issues:

- The total number of competing outlets a market can support.

- The number of your stores a market can support before cannibalization (stealing of customers from one of your stores by another) occurs. This is often determined by analyzing your trading area and calculating how many locations would be optimal given the trading area size and the total size of the market (total market size divided by trading area size).

- The number of stores required for mass media such as newspapers, television, and radio to be efficiently leveraged, making the media affordable for your company from a percent of market sales or sales per store standpoint.

Questions

- Where do consumers shop for products in your category? Where do they shop for your company's product? What channel or outlet type do consumers use most when purchasing?

- What is the importance of department stores, supermarkets, specialty stores, chain stores, independents, direct mail, discount stores, or other types of outlets that sell your product category or product? What are the sales trends of each outlet type used by your product category (five-year trend)?

- What channels or methods of distribution are receiving increased use by the industry? Are new channels emerging? What trends are noticeable in the stores that dominate the sales of your product category?

- What channels or methods of distribution does your competition use? If they use different channels from you, why?

- Do you have adequate penetration of outlets to maximize sales in any given market?

- Does expansion into new territories make sense? Are there additional areas of the country where you should be doing business?

- Does your product require mass, selective, or exclusive distribution? Why? Does it require a combination of distribution methods? Who can best provide this type of distribution? What about your competitors' products; do they require mass, selective, or exclusive distribution?

Package Goods

A package goods company views distribution differently from a retailer. Package goods companies sell to outlets, which in turn sell to consumers. A cereal company sells to grocery stores who in turn sell to consumers. Unlike retailers, package goods companies don't own the channel of distribution; thus, there is more emphasis placed on making sure the package goods product is accepted and sold into the channel and receives proper shelf space and merchandising support relative to competitors' products.

Channel Type/Trends. The package goods marketer has to determine the type of channel(s) best suited for the product. For example, it may be chain grocery stores, independent grocery stores, mass merchandisers, specialty stores, or convenience stores.

Market Coverage. As with retailing, you need to determine the number of outlets required to cover a trading area efficiently. But since the package goods firm doesn't own the outlets, there is less concern with penetration. In some cases, the goal is to reach 100 percent market coverage of grocery store outlets in a given market. At the other extreme, some manufacturers offer exclusive distribution to a chain in return for greater sales and merchandising support. In still other situations, the product is distributed on a more limited basis to outlets that are consistent with the image of the product.

In most cases, package goods marketers do not refer to distribution coverage in terms of total stores. Distribution is referred to as the percentage of total grocery store dollar volume that the stores carrying the marketer's product account for in all grocery commodities, or all commodity volume (ACV). Thus the term 65 percent ACV means that the marketer's brand is carried by grocery stores doing 65 percent of all commodity grocery store volume.

Shelf Space. The amount of shelf space a product receives is critical to how well the product will do from a sales standpoint. Limited shelf space and poor positioning on the shelf are both reasons for concern and need to be corrected.

Geography. As with retail, the package goods marketer should analyze the geographic territories of the firm's distribution to determine if there are markets that should be further penetrated or new markets that should be entered.

Sales Method. An integral part of package goods distribution is the personal selling method. Some companies choose to use an in-house sales force, others use independent sales representatives and brokers, and still others use distributors or wholesalers. You should analyze your current method as well as what your competitors use and then decide the best method or combination of methods for your company.

Another issue to be explored is the selling programs your company has in place to sell the trade. The questions referring to this topic are designed to establish the importance of trade deals, cooperative advertising, and other allowances in your marketplace.

Questions

- Where do consumers shop for products in your category? Where do they shop for your company's product? What channel or outlet type do consumers use most when purchasing?

- What is the importance of department stores, supermarkets, convenience stores, mass merchandisers, specialty stores, chain stores, independents, direct mail, discount stores, or other types of outlets that sell your product category or product? What are the sales trends of each outlet type used by your product category (five-year trend)?

- What channels or methods of distribution are receiving increased use by the industry? Are new channels emerging? What trends are noticeable in the stores that dominate the sales of your product category?

- What channels or methods of distribution does your competition use? If they use different channels from you, why?

- Do you have enough market coverage to maximize sales in any given market?

- What is the ACV in each of your company's markets? What is the ACV for each of your major competitors in those same markets?

- Is the percentage of shelf space your product receives in major outlets greater, the same, or lower than your competitors'?

- Does expansion into new territories make sense? Are there additional areas of the country where you should be doing business?

- Does your product require mass, selective, or exclusive distribution? Why? Does it require a combination of distribution methods? Who can best provide this type of distribution? What about your competitors' products; do they require mass, selective, or exclusive distribution?

- How many potential dealers, wholesalers, distributors, brokers, or retail outlets are there? What are their distribution trading areas geographically?

- How do you sell your product to the trade or other businesses? Do you use in-house sales staff, independent representatives, wholesalers, or distributors? What is the most efficient method of selling to distributors, wholesalers, or the retail trade?

- What is the importance of your product to the retail stores or distribution channel that sells it? Do you need the channel's services more than they need your product? Who has the channel power? How important is your product to the channel in terms of profit or volume (units and dollars)? Does it help build or sustain traffic? Is it prestigious? Does it help sell other goods? How do these points differ from your competition?

- How do retailers or other distributors sell or market your product? Does your product receive aggressive sales support, or does your product have to sell itself? Does your product receive prominent display relative to the competition? Does your product get promoted in-store or to the ultimate purchaser by the distribution channel? Does your product receive the same merchandising and promotion support (more or less) relative to the competition? Does your product receive other promotion, advertising, or merchandising support?

- How established is your product with the trade? How well is it known and accepted by the trade? Is it important to them? Do you receive cooperation from the channels you sell to? (Same for your competition.)

- What is the minimum order size you require of your customers/channels? Is this standard in your industry? What are the payment terms? How often is restocking needed?

- Do storage, price marking, packaging, or accounting practices help sell the trade or create problems?

- Do quantity discounts, cooperative advertising, promotion allowances, price discounts, trade promotions, or other deals play a large role in the selling of your product category to the trade? How? Does your company have the same programs your competitors do?

- What is the customary markup of your product by the trade? Does this affect your marketing to the trade or the acceptance of your product by the end consumer?

- Are retail sales or sales to the trade subject to taxes or legal restrictions?

- What are the stocking requirements of the trade? How does your company make allocation decisions? Who gets the best fill rates and why? How are out of stocks handled?

- When and how often are the orders placed and by whom?

Business-to-Business

Business-to-business firms either sell directly to other businesses or through channels such as wholesalers or distributors, or both.

Channel Types/Trends. The business-to-business firm must decide the most efficient and effective channel method for the company. We did a business review for a national manufacturer of sinks and disposals that clearly demonstrated the trend of more and more do-it-yourselfers installing their own sinks and disposals. Further study demonstrated that a shift in purchasing patterns had accompanied the strength of do-it-yourselfers in the marketplace; home centers and lumberyards were now selling more of this type of product than traditional plumbing channels. Thus, because of the channel trend section of the business review, selling emphasis was placed against home centers and lumberyards, with a new channel of distribution established for the manufacturer.

Geography. The same issues need to be addressed here as were discussed in the package goods section.

Personal Selling Method. As with package goods firms, business-to-business companies must decide how to sell the product through the distribution channels. Company sales representatives, independent sales representatives, or wholesalers/distributors all have advantages and disadvantages. Remember, in the business review, your job is to analyze which method is used most successfully within the industry, as well as by your company and your competitors.

As with the package goods section, the business-to-business firm must also address the issues of sales programs to the channels. The importance of deals, allowances, co-op advertising, and other sales program issues are detailed in the questions.

Questions

- What channels or methods of distribution are receiving increased use by the industry? Are new channels emerging? What trends are noticeable?

- What channels or methods of distribution does your competition use? If they use different channels from you, why?

- Do you have enough market coverage to maximize sales in any given market?

- Does expansion into new territories make sense? Are there additional areas of the country where you should be doing business?

- Does your product require mass, selective, or exclusive distribution? Why? Does it require a combination of distribution methods? Who can best provide this type of distribution? What about your competitors' products; do they require mass, selective, or exclusive distribution?

- How many potential dealers, wholesalers, distributors, retail outlets, or other business customers are there? What are their distribution trading areas geographically?

- How do you sell your product to the trade or other businesses? Do you use in-house sales staff, independent representatives, wholesalers, or distributors? What is the most efficient method of selling to distributors, wholesalers, the retail trade, or other business customers?

- What is the importance of your product to your business customers, the retail stores, or distribution channel that sells it? Do you need the channel's services more than they need your product? Who has the channel power? How important is your product to the channel in terms of profit or volume (units and dollars)? Does it help build or sustain traffic? Is it prestigious? Does it help sell other goods? How do these points differ from your competition?

- How do retailers or other distributors sell or market your product? Does your product receive aggressive sales support or does your product have to sell itself? Does your product get promoted to the ultimate purchaser by the distribution channel? Does your product receive the same merchandising and promotion support (less or more) relative to the competition? Does your product receive other promotion, advertising, or merchandising support?

- How established is your product with the trade? How well is it known and accepted by the trade? Is it important to them? Do you receive cooperation from the channels you sell to? (Same for your competition.)

- What is the minimum order size you require of your customers/channels? Is this standard in your industry? What are the payment terms? How often is restocking needed?

- Do storage, price marking, packaging, or accounting practices help sell the trade or create problems?

- Do quantity discounts, cooperative advertising, promotion allowances, price discounts, trade promotions, or other deals play a large role in the selling of your product category to the trade? How? Does your company have the same programs your competitors do?

- What is the customary markup of your product by the trade? Does this affect your marketing to the trade or the acceptance of your product by the end consumer? Are sales subject to taxes or legal restrictions?

- What are the stocking requirements of the trade? How does your company make allocation decisions? Who gets the best fill rates and why? How are out of stocks handled?

- When and how often are the orders placed and by whom?

Service Firms

The service industry's method of distribution is much like the retailer's. It encompasses the business's office and how the service is sold to customers.

Type of Office. Of consideration for the service business is the type of office used to sell the service. For a service company, one of the only tangible things associated with the company is the actual office. Therefore, the office becomes an important representation of the more intangible service being sold. For many services, the service itself is sold or delivered out of the office. In this case, how and where the service is sold and delivered must be closely analyzed.

Geography. An important decision is where to locate an office or offices within a given market. When The Hiebing Group first began operation, we wanted to be close to Madison's Capitol Square because of the positive image associated with being downtown, adjacent to the center of state government, and close to the University of Wisconsin. When we outgrew our first location, we decided to stay close to downtown and the university, while maintaining a positive creative image. We found a historic mansion overlooking Lake Mendota, close to downtown, achieving our goals and creating an office environment and image consistent with that of the agency.

Another issue to be addressed is the number of markets in which you do business. Which markets seem ripe for geographic expansion, and which ones are not currently profitable and may need to be abandoned?

Penetration. As with retailers, proximity is also important to firms providing service. Accordingly, service companies also must decide how many locations and sales and/or service people are needed to cover any given market effectively and efficiently.

Questions

- Where do consumers for services in your category shop?

- What are the current methods of delivery used for services in your category? Are new methods of delivery emerging? Are there noticeable trends among the firms that dominate your service category?

- How does your competition deliver their services? If they use different delivery methods from you, why?

- Does expansion into new territories make sense? Are there additional areas of the country where you should be doing business?

- Does your product require mass, selective, or exclusive distribution? Why? Does it require a combination of delivery methods? Who can best provide this new method of delivery? What about your competitors—do they require different methods of delivery?

- Is the best way to deliver your service through company owned offices, franchisers, or dealerships?

- What type of office is most consistent with your company's image? Describe the office interiors/exteriors of your competitors; are they similar to or different from yours? Where, when, and how is your service best sold to consumers?

Step 8: Pricing

Price is a prominent part of the marketing decision making process. A price that is too high may discourage purchase of the product and encourage competition in the form of lower price and more entries into the product category. Alternatively, a price that is too low may be a deterrent to reaching profit and sales goals.

The business review section on pricing is designed to provide pricing data relating to competition, changes in the marketplace price structure, and strengths of consumer demand. This information will provide a reference to help guide your pricing objectives and strategies in the subsequent marketing plan.

The business review should provide you with four major insights on pricing:

- The price of your product/brands relative to the competition.

- Your company's sales by price point relative to the competition.

- The price elasticity of your product. (A price elastic product is one for which, if the price is raised, sales go down, and if the price is lowered, sales go up. A price inelastic product is one for which, even when the price is increased or decreased, sales are not affected positively or negatively to the degree they are with a price elastic product.)

- The cost structure of your product.

Questions
Price of Your Product

- What is the pricing structure for the product category? Are there price point products, brands, or stores that sell for less than yours? Is there a range from premium to off-price/discount pricing in your industry?

- What is the pricing structure for your product relative to the competition? Does the relationship of your product's price to that of the competition change during different selling seasons?

- In addition to pure price, are discounts, credit, promotional allowances, return policies, restocking charges, shipping policies, etc., important to the ultimate sale of your product?

Sales by Price Point

- What is the distribution of sales by price point for your industry and your company (five-year trend)? Do most sales fall in one price category, or can consumers be segmented by price point?

- What has been the trend in pricing (five-year trend)? Are there price segments that are growing or shrinking?

Price Elasticity

- How price elastic is your product category? When you raise and/or lower the price, how does it affect demand? Are consumers price sensitive to your product category?

- Where is your product priced in relation to your major competitors? Why is it priced where it is?

Cost Structure

- What does it cost to produce your product, obtain the product for sale, or provide the service?

- What is the gross margin on your product? What are the corresponding selling and marketing costs? For each item sold or hour of service provided, what is the contribution to fixed costs and overhead (gross margin less direct selling costs)?

Step 9: Historical Marketing Review of Your Company versus the Competition

This competitive analysis section is designed to provide you with a summary of how your company is performing as compared to the competition across key marketing variables. This phase forces you to consider strategic and tactical differences and similarities between how your company markets its product(s) and how the competition markets their product(s). An analysis of your company's marketing activities in relation to the competition can provide *benchmark information* necessary to prepare your marketing plan in Steps Three through Ten. This knowledge will provide insights into potential defensive or offensive strategies that you can include in the marketing plan to curtail or exploit a major competitor's strength or weakness. In addition, by thoroughly studying your past marketing efforts and those of the competition, you may look at successes and failures in a new light. There might be ways to modify some of your competitors' more successful programs and make them your own, or there might be changes that can be made to successful programs that will make them even better.

How to Develop Competitive Information

You must analyze your company and your competitors in terms of sales, target market, positioning, marketing objectives and strategies, positioning, product/branding/packaging, pricing, distribution, personal selling techniques, promotion strategies and expenditures, customer service, merchandising, and publicity. Attempt to review the previous three years, as well as projecting into the future. Past years' successes and failures for both your company and your competitors can be great learning tools.

You should also consider the results of your marketing testing or marketing research and development (R&D) program. Did you introduce any new products, line extensions, services, new merchandise, or store concepts? Did you test different approaches in your advertising message? Did you test the use of new and/or investment spending? Did you test various promotional offers? What can you learn from past tests that can be translated into future success? If you have been doing the same things year after year, you should explore new uses of your marketing tools to ensure a competitive edge that will help guarantee increased sales and profits year after year.

Competitive analyses are not easy to complete because it is often difficult to obtain specific information about competitors. However, there are many secondary sources available—from the census to trade publications and independent research studies. Media representatives are also a source of information. In addition, we encourage you to shop your competition by purchasing your competitors' products.

Finally, one of the best ways to obtain competitive information is through awareness, attitude, and behavior primary research. If your company uses market tracking surveys, you can determine trends of the following:

- Awareness levels of competitors relative to your company.

- Consumers' rating of key product attributes for your company relative to the competition.

- Market share estimates for competitors relative to your company.

- Purchase ratios/trial and repeat purchases for your product relative to the competition.

- Shopping habits for your product versus the competition (normally shop first, etc.).

Questions

Whenever possible, develop answers for the past three years and project responses for the upcoming year.

Market Share/Sales

- What are the market share and sales of your competitors? Have they been growing or declining? How do their market share and sales compare to yours?

- How have your marketing programs affected market share and sales over the past five years? Have they been successful compared to those of your competition?

Target Market

- Whom do your competitors sell to? What is the description of their target markets? Are they the same as yours? If they are different, how do they differ?

Marketing Objectives and Strategies

- Summarize the major marketing objectives and strategies of your company and those of your competitors. How are they similar, different?

Positioning

- What is the positioning of your company and your company's competitors? Is your positioning unique? Do you have a strong positioning relative to your competitors?

- Is your positioning dominating a strong attribute that is important to your target market?

Product/Branding/Packaging Strengths and Weaknesses

- What products do your competitors sell? How do these products differ from yours? What are the strengths and weaknesses of your product? What are your competitors' products' strengths and weaknesses? How do your product and your competitors' products rate on product attributes that are important to the consumer? Answer the same questions pertaining to branding (product name) and packaging.

Pricing

- What is the price of your product compared to that of your competitors? Is your pricing structure the same, higher, or lower?

Distribution/Store Penetration/Market Coverage

- Does your company use the same distribution channels as your competitors? What are the strengths and weaknesses of your distribution methods versus your competitors'?

- If you are a retailer, what are the penetration levels of stores for your company versus that of your competition? If you are a manufacturer, what is the market coverage of your product? Is it sufficient? How does it compare to that of your competitors?

- Where is your product sold? Where are your competitors' products sold?

Personal Selling

- What was your sales performance last year? Did you meet your goals?

- How does your company's selling philosophy differ from that of your competitors? Are there different methods you may want to consider in the future? If so, why?

Promotion

- What were the results of your company's promotions and those of your competitors last year? What was successful or unsuccessful? Why? How do your company's promotions differ from those of your competitors?

- What promotions do your competition execute that are particularly successful?

Advertising Message

- How does your advertising compare to your competitors'? Is it similar or different? What is the message of your advertising versus those of your major competitors?

- How successful has your advertising been relative to your competitors' advertising? What are the strengths and weaknesses of your advertising and that of your competitors?

Media Strategy and Expenditures

- Where, when, and how do you and your competitors use the media?

- What is the media spending in total and by medium for your company and your competitors? Do you dominate any one medium? Where are your competitors the strongest?

Customer Service Policies

- What are your company's customer service policies? Do they differ from the competition's? If so, how?

Merchandising

- What is the merchandising philosophy of your competitors? Are you unique or is your merchandising similar to the competition? Does your merchandising help to communicate your positioning?

Publicity

- Do you have an active publicity program? Does your competition? How much publicity did your product receive versus competitive products?

Testing/Marketing R&D

- What tests did your company and the competition execute in the past year? Were they successful? What did you learn from the tests?

Summary of Strengths and Weaknesses

- Based on the information above, what are the strengths and weaknesses of your company compared to each major competitor?

Step 10: Demand Analysis

The last step in the business review is to attempt to calculate demand for your product. The conclusions will be directional and are intended to provide you with a rough estimate of the size of your market and the potential business you might generate. It should give you a check to make sure the sales goals you set later in the plan are realistic and obtainable.

How to Estimate Demand for Your Product

The following outlines the procedures to take in estimating demand for your product.

1. *Target Market.* Define the target market in terms of numbers of potential customers. For example, if your going-in target market is women age 25 to 49, provide the total number of women age 25 to 49. This is the top level figure of potential customers. It can be used for calculating future or potential demand.

2. *Geographic Territory.* Define your geographic territory and determine the number of your target market in this area. You can do this by utilizing the Standard Rate and Data Service (SRDS) or the Nielsen Test Market Profile Resource. Or you can calculate the percentage of the total population the target market constitutes and multiply it by the total number of people in your geographic territory. Whichever method you use, the end result should be an estimate of the number of target market customers in your geographic territory.

3. *Consumption Constraints.* Determine whether there are consumption constraints that will reduce the target market for your product. For example, apartment dwellers have no need for garden tools or lawn mowers. From this review, develop a final estimate of customers in your geographic territory.

4. *Average Purchase per Year per Customer.* Determine the number of purchases per year. From the business review and the purchase rates/ buying habits section, you should have estimates of the average number of purchases per year for your product category.

5. *Total Purchase per Year in Category.* Multiply the number of customers in your territory by the average number of purchases per year to get total purchases.

6. *Average Price.* Determine the average price of your product using the pricing section of the business review.

7. *Total Dollar Purchases.* Multiply the total purchases from Number 5 by the average price in Number 6 to determine total dollar purchases.

8. *Your Company's Market Share of Purchase.* Review market share data and trends from the sales analysis section, and competitive market shares and strengths and weaknesses from the competitive analysis section of your business review. Also, consider loyalty measures from the purchase rates/buying habits section of the business review. Multiply your market share by the total in Number 7. Adjust this number up or down depending on the increases or decreases of your company's market share versus the competition over the past five years. (For example, if your company has been losing 5 percent market share per year over five years, project this average loss into your market share projection).

9. *Additional Factors.* Additional factors that correlate to the demand for your product, such as the state of the economy, demographic fluctuations, changing consumer tastes and lifestyles, etc., should be analyzed for their effect on demand. The influence on demand of rising or falling interest rates should be analyzed if your product is extremely interest rate sensitive and there is good probability that interest rates will rise or fall within the next year. Likewise, if your product's sales are teen oriented, determine whether the number of teens is growing or shrinking and project the effect this will have on sales. Based on this information, subjectively adjust the final figure you derived in Number 8. At this point you should have a fairly reasonable estimate of your company's potential share of total dollars and customers.

Further subjective analysis should be done utilizing information developed in the business review, such as competitive factors, store location and analysis, competitive advertising expenditures, store loyalty, and the future economic factors affecting purchases to provide input on final adjustments up or down of the demand expectation generated in the above calculations.

Questions

- How many consumers are there in your target market nationally?

- How many consumers are in your defined trading area or geographic market territory?

- What consumption habits are there that limit the potential customer base of your target market?

- What is the average number of purchases of your product per year?

- What is the total number of purchases by the target market in your geographic territory per year?

- What is the average price of your product?

- What are the total dollar purchases of your product category in your geographic target market?

- What is your company's market share? Is it trending up or down?

- What competitive factors will affect your market share or your chances to increase your market share?

- What additional factors are there that strongly affect demand for your product? How will recent or expected changes in these factors change demand for your product? Why?

WRITING STYLE

Now that you have answered the questions in each section and completed the charts, it is best to summarize the important findings from each section. This is helpful for two reasons:

1. It is much easier to develop problems and opportunities (as you'll be doing in Chapter 3) if the business review has been condensed and summarized.

2. The summary statements provide a good management summary and support during presentations.

We recommend developing summary statements for each section of the business review. They should precede each section, serving as a management summary when the final business review is ready for presentation. Your summary statements should be objective. This is no place for developing strategy. Keep the statements concise and focused on reporting the facts. Include summary rationale when needed. Examples summarizing major findings for a canning company would be as follows.

Summary Statement Examples

Buying Habits. Canned vegetables are used by a high percentage (80 percent) of households. Canned vegetables are a relatively high usage category. Fifty-nine percent of female homemakers use 4 or more cans per month. Twenty-nine percent use 10 or more cans per month. Thirteen percent use 16 or more cans per month.

Target Market. Canned vegetable consumption is dominated by medium and heavy users. Thirty-seven percent of canned good female purchasers account for over 65 percent of the canned vegetables used per month.

Sales. While the canned tomato category has increased dramatically (140 percent) for the industry over the past five years, Company X has experienced only moderate growth (20 percent). This is far below the industry growth pattern.

Worksheet 2.1

Demographic Profile by Volume Step 2: Review of the Consumer Target Market

Demographic Descriptor	Percent of Total Population (Total Population Number)	Percent of Total Purchases (Total Dollar or Unit Volume)	Relative Volume Index: Purchases/Population
Age			
Under 18			
18 to 24			
25 to 34			
35 to 44			
45 to 54			
55+			
Sex			
Male			
Female			
Household Income			
$15,000 and under			
$15,001 to $24,000			
$24,001 to $30,000			
$30,001 to $40,000			
$40,001 to $50,000			
$50,001 to $60,000			
$60,000+			
Education			
Did not graduate high school			
Graduated high school			
Some college			
Graduated college			
Occupation			
White-collar			
Blue-collar			
Farmer			
Employment			
Full-time			
Part-time			
Unemployed			
Family Size			
1			
2			
3 to 4			
5 to 6			
7+			
Geography			
Urban			
Surburban			
Rural			
Home			
Own home			
Rent			

Where to Find This Information
SMRB (Simmons Market Research Bureau)
MRI (Mediamark Research, Inc.)
Fairchild Fact Files
Census data/county business patterns
Industry trade publication research departments
Industry research studies (supplied through trade associations)

Worksheet 2.2

Demographic Description of Company Purchasers Compared to Category Purchasers Step 2: Review of the Consumer Target Market

Demographic Descriptor	Percent Purchasers of Product Nationally ( )*	Percent Purchasers of Company Product ( )*	Index: Company/ National Purchasers
Age			
Under 18			
18 to 24			
25 to 34			
35 to 44			
45 to 54			
55+			
Sex			
Male			
Female			
Household Income			
$15,000 and under			
$15,001 to $24,000			
$24,001 to $30,000			
$30,001 to $40,000			
$40,001 to $50,000			
$50,001+			
Education			
Did not graduate high school			
Graduated high school			
Some college			
Graduated college			
Occupation			
White-collar			
Blue-collar			
Farmer			
Employment			
Full-time			
Part-time			
Unemployed			
Family Size			
1			
2			
3 to 4			
5 to 6			
7+			
Geography			
Urban			
Suburban			
Rural			
Home			
Own home			
Rent			

*Provide total dollar volume in parentheses.

Where to Find This Information
SMRB (Simmons Market Research Bureau)
MRI (Mediamark Research, Inc.)
Your company records
Primary research

	Heavy User Demographic Profile	**Total Demographic Profile**
Age		
Sex		
Household income		
Education		
Employment		
Family size		
Geography		
Home ownership		

Lifestyle Description of the Heavy User Compared to the Average User

Where to Find This Information
SMRB (Simmons Market Research Bureau)
MRI (Mediamark Research, Inc.)
Your company records
Primary research

Worksheet 2.4

This chart demonstrates the total number of businesses that *exist nationally* and categorizes those businesses by SIC category. It also delineates the number of businesses by SIC by employment size and dollar volume.

SIC	Total Establishments	
	Number	**Percent of Total Census**
Agriculture/Forestry/Fisheries		
Mining		
Construction		
Manufacturing		
Transportation		
Public Utilities		
Wholesale Trade		
Retail Trade		
Finance/Insurance/Real Estate Services		
Public Administration		
Percent		
Total Census		

Where to Find This Information
County Business Patterns, U.S. Department of Commerce, Bureau of the Census
Dun's Marketing Service, a company of the Dun & Bradstreet Corporation

Worksheet 2.5

This chart demonstrates the total number of customers a firm has and categorizes those businesses by SIC category. The SIC categories could be further broken out if necessary (e.g., sporting good retailers versus the overall category of retailers). It also delineates the number of businesses by SIC of number of employees and dollar volume. This chart can then be compared with the previous one to determine company penetration of each SIC category.

SIC	Company Customers	
	Number	**Percent of Total Customers**
Agriculture/Forestry/Fisheries		
Mining		
Construction		
Manufacturing		
Transportation		
Public Utilities		
Wholesale Trade		
Retail Trade		
Finance/Insurance/Real Estate Services		
Public Administration		
Percent		
Total Customers		

Where to Find This Information
Company data

Percent of Establishments by Employment Size Class						Percent of Establishments by Dollar Volume ($MM)					
1 to 4	5 to 9	10 to 19	20 to 49	50 to 99	100+	000 to 1	2 to 9	10 to 49	50 to 99	100 to 499	500+

Percent of Establishments by Employment Size Class						Percent of Establishments by Dollar Volume ($MM)					
1 to 4	5 to 9	10 to 19	20 to 49	50 to 99	100+	000 to 1	2 to 9	10 to 49	50 to 99	100 to 499	500+

Worksheet 2.6

Revenue Distribution of Clients by SIC Category Step 3: Review of the Business-to-Business Target Market

This chart details the total revenue and average revenue per customer by SIC segment. It also provides a comparison of total sales and average sales per customer across the SIC segments.

SIC	Number of Customers	Total Company Sales per SIC Category	Average $ per Client ($M)	Index to Average (Average $ per Client/Average $ per Client All Categories)	Index to Average (Total Sales per SIC Category/Average $ All Categories)
Agriculture/Forestry/Fisheries					
Mining					
Construction					
Manufacturing					
Transportation					
Public Utilities					
Wholesale Trade					
Retail Trade					
Finance/Insurance/Real Estate Services					
Public Administration					
Total					
Average All Categories					

Where to Find This Information
Trade publications
Company records

Worksheet 2.7

Product Category Purchases by Outlet Type (If more relevant than SIC segmenting) Step 3: Review of the Business-to-Business Target Market

Outlet Type	Where Consumers Purchase	Percent of Total Purchases

Where to Find This Information
Trade publications
Industry sources

Worksheet 2.8

National Distribution of Businesses by Size by State by SIC
Step 3: Review of the Business-to-Business Target Market

This chart demonstrates the total number of businesses that exist by state and categorizes those businesses by SIC category. This provides a clear demand picture on a statewide basis, or even county by county if necessary, enabling analysis of demand potential within more narrowly defined geographic trading areas. A chart for each state would be constructed.

SIC	Total Establishments	
	Number	Percent of Total Census
Agriculture/Forestry/Fisheries		
Mining		
Construction		
Manufacturing		
Transportation		
Public Utilities		
Wholesale Trade		
Retail Trade		
Finance/Insurance/Real Estate Services		
Public Administration		
Percent		
Total Census		

Where to Find This Information
County Business Patterns, U.S. Department of Commerce, Bureau of the Census
Dun's Marketing Service, a company of the Dun & Bradstreet Corporation

Worksheet 2.9

Company Distribution of Customers by Size by State by SIC
Step 3: Review of the Business-to-Business Target Market

This chart allows for a comparison of company business with the total potential business in the marketplace. Through utilizing the previous chart, the marketer can determine penetration of clients and focus emphasis against areas of high potential. A chart for each state would be constructed.

SIC	Company Customers	
	Number	Percent of Total Customers
Agriculture/Forestry/Fisheries		
Mining		
Construction		
Manufacturing		
Transportation		
Public Utilities		
Wholesale Trade		
Retail Trade		
Finance/Insurance/Real Estate Services		
Public Administration		
Percent		
Total Customers		

Where to Find This Information
Company data

Percent of Establishments by Employment Size Class						Percent of Establishments by Dollar Volume ($MM)					
1 to 4	5 to 9	10 to 19	20 to 49	50 to 99	100+	000 to 1	2 to 9	10 to 49	50 to 99	100 to 499	500+

Percent of Establishments by Employment Size Class						Percent of Establishments by Dollar Volume ($MM)					
1 to 4	5 to 9	10 to 19	20 to 49	50 to 99	100+	000 to 1	2 to 9	10 to 49	50 to 99	100 to 499	500+

Worksheet 2.10

Sales Seasonality by Month Step 4: Sales Analysis

Month	Company Percentage of Sales	Company Index to Average ( )	Industry Percentage of Sales	Industry Index to Average ( )
January				
February				
March				
April				
May				
June				
July				
August				
September				
October				
November				
December				

Where to Find This Information
Fairchild Fact Files
Company data

Worksheet 2.11

Brand Seasonality by Month Step 4: Sales Analysis

	Base*	November		December		Etc.
		Percent of Total Dollars	Index to Total Year	Percent of Total Dollars	Index to Total Year	
Company Brand X	%			%		
Company Brand Y						
Company Brand Z						

*Base equals total figures for the year.

Where to Find This Information
Company data

Worksheet 2.12

Product Category Purchase Rates by Geographic Market
Step 6: Purchase Rates/Buying Habits

DMA	Percent of U.S. Population	Percent of Product Dollar Volume	Category Development Index: (Volume/ Population)	Population Number (000)	Dollar Volume of Product Category Nationally ($000)	Per Capita Consumption
City 1	%	%			$	$
City 2						
City 3						
City 4						

Where to Find This Information
Sales & Marketing Management Survey of Buying Power

Worksheet 2.13

Company Purchase Rates by Geographic Market Step 6: Purchase Rates/Buying Habits

DMA	Percent of U.S. Population	Percent of Dollar Volume	Brand Development Index: (Volume/ Population)	Population Number (000)	Dollar Volume Company (000)	Per Capita Consumption
City 1	%	%			$	$
City 2						
City 3						
City 4						

Where to Find This Information
Company data

Worksheet 2.14

Trading Areas by Store Step 6: Purchase Rates/Buying Habits

Zip Codes Surrounding Store	Percent of Customers Over 1 Week Period
	%

Where to Find This Information
Company store survey
Company mailing lists

Worksheet 2.15
Brand Loyalty Step 6: Purchase Rates/Buying Habits

Brand	All	Sole	Loyalty Index	Sole and Primary	Loyalty Index	All Users
	%	%		%		%

Where to Find This Information
SMRB (Simmons Market Research Bureau)
MRI (Mediamark Research, Inc.)
Primary research

Worksheet 2.16
Purchasing Rates/Buying Habits Step 6: Purchase Rates/Buying Habits

This chart provides examples of what can be achieved through this type of primary research. A "heavy purchasers" and an "all purchasers" category is provided for each question.

Number of (whatever the product category) purchased in one year.

    Heavy purchasers   _____

    Purchasers   _____

Number of stores usually visited to find what you want per purchase.

    Heavy purchasers   _____

    Purchasers   _____

Amount purchased per visit (dollars and units).

    Heavy users   _____

    Users   _____

Visits to *your store* per month/year.

    Heavy purchasers   _____

    Purchasers   _____

Visits to *all stores* per month/year.

    Heavy purchasers   _____

    Purchasers   _____

Purchases at *your store* per month/year.

    Heavy purchasers   _____

    Purchasers   _____

Purchases at all stores per month/year.

    Heavy purchasers   _____

    Purchasers   _____

Average purchase ratio in percentage of people who purchase versus those who do not with each visit to the store.

    Heavy users   _____

    Users   _____

Where to Find This Information
In-store survey

Worksheet 2.17

Trial/Retrial Step 6: Purchase Rates/Buying Habits

Brand	Percent Ever Used	Percent Used Last 6 Months or Categorized as Regular User	Loyalty Measure: Percent Used Past 6 Months/Percent Ever Used
Company X			
A			
B			
Competition			
C			
D			
E			
F			

Where to Find This Information
Market survey

Worksheet 2.18

Purchases by Outlet Type (Five-Year Trend) Step 7: Distribution

Distribution Outlet Type	Total Sales				Points Change 1989 to 1993	
	1989		1993			
	Units	Dollars	Units	Dollars	Units	Dollars
	%	%	%	%	%	%

Where to Find This Information
Fairchild Fact Files
Trade publications

Worksheet 2.19   Market Coverage Chart   Step 7: Distribution

Coverage for Your Product	Percent of Total Product Business in Market % ACV	Percent of Shelf Space Given Your Product in Store	Percent Shelf Space for Main Competitors in Product Category	
			Competitor 1	Competitor 2
Outlet A	%	%	%	%
Outlet B				
Outlet C				
Outlet D				
Outlet E				
Outlet F				
Outlet G				
Outlet H				
Outlet I				

Note: An identical chart would be created for each key market.

Where to Find This Information
Store checks/interviews with store managers
Nielsen
SAMI

Worksheet 2.20   Price of Your Company's Product Relative to the Competition during Key Selling Periods   Step 8: Pricing

	Price 1st Quarter	Price 2nd Quarter	Price 3rd Quarter	Price 4th Quarter
Your Company				
Competitor A				
Competitor B				
Competitor C				
Competitor D				

Where to Find This Information
Company data

	Price Range Product Category		Price Range Company's Product	
	Percent of Sales	**Percent of Items**	**Percent of Sales**	**Percent of Items**
1993				
$ to $				
$ to $				
$ to $				
$ to $				
$ to $				
$ to $				
1992				
$ to $				
$ to $				
$ to $				
$ to $				
$ to $				
$ to $				
1991				
$ to $				
$ to $				
$ to $				
$ to $				
$ to $				
$ to $				
1990 etc.				
1989 etc.				

Where to Find This Information
Fairchild Fact Files
Company data
Trade publications

Worksheet 2.22

Annual Competitive Spending Analysis Step 9: Historical Marketing
Review

Competitor	Total Dollar Expenditures $	Share of Spending— Total Expenditures %	Change from Last Year %	Television			Newspaper		
				Total Dollar Expenditures $	Percent %	Change from Last Year %	Total Dollar Expenditures $	Percent %	Change from Last Year %

Note: The above information should also be obtained on a *quarterly basis* to track seasonality of spending. If available, total dollars for each category should also be obtained.

Where to Find This Information

Media representatives from television stations, newspapers, radio stations, outdoor companies
LNA (leading national advertisers) for national companies
PIB
RADAR
Media records
BAR

Magazine			Radio			Outdoor		
Total Dollar Expenditures	Percent	Change from Last Year	Total Dollar Expenditures	Percent	Change from Last Year	Total Dollar Expenditures	Percent	Change from Last Year
$	%	%	$	%	%	$	%	%

Worksheet 2.23

Competitive Analysis   Step 9: Historical Marketing Review

Your Company	Competitor A	Competitor B	Competitor C	Competitor D

Market Share/Sales
Current
Growth/Decline Past 5 Years

Target Market
Primary
Secondary

Marketing Objectives/Strategies

Positioning

Product/Branding/Packaging
Strengths
Weaknesses

Pricing Strategies/Pricing Structure

**Distribution/Store Penetration/
Market Coverage Strategy**

Geographic Sales Territory

Store/Outlet
Locations and description of locations
(e.g., for retailers, strip center, mall, etc.)

Personal Selling Strategies

Promotion Strategies

Advertising Message

Media Strategies and Expenditures
TV
Radio
Newspaper
Outdoor
Direct mail
Other

Customer Service Policies

Merchandising Strategies

Publicity Strategies

Testing/Marketing R&D Strategies

Summary of Strengths and Weaknesses

Where to Find This Information
Your company's past experiences
Primary research
Fairchild Fact Files
Trade publications
Industry 10-K reports
Media representatives
Field sales reps
Radio/TV reports

Worksheet 2.24

Demand Potential Step 10: Demand Analysis

1. **Target Market**
   DMA population
   Target market

2. **Geographic Territory**
   Target market in store trading area

3. **Consumption Constraints**

4. **Average Purchases per Year per Customer**

5. **Total Purchases per Year in Category**

6. **Average Price**

7. **Total Dollar Purchases per Year**

8. **Your Company's Share of Purchases**
   Estimated market share of ––––––––––––––––––––

9. **Additional Factors**

Final Demand Expectations for Your Company

Where to Find This Information
Business review

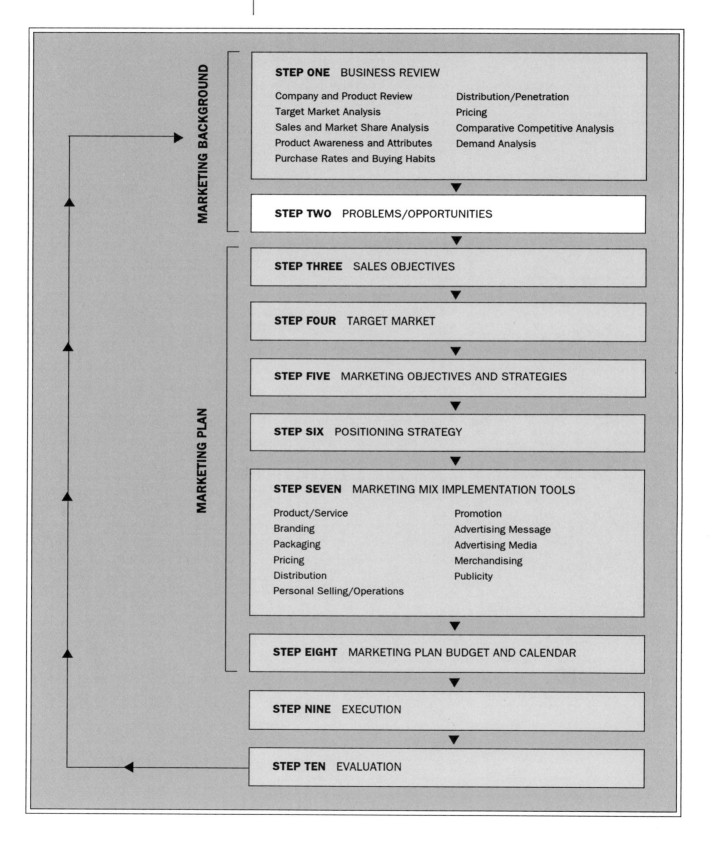

MARKETING BACKGROUND

STEP ONE BUSINESS REVIEW

Company and Product Review
Target Market Analysis
Sales and Market Share Analysis
Product Awareness and Attributes
Purchase Rates and Buying Habits

Distribution/Penetration
Pricing
Comparative Competitive Analysis
Demand Analysis

STEP TWO PROBLEMS/OPPORTUNITIES

MARKETING PLAN

STEP THREE SALES OBJECTIVES

STEP FOUR TARGET MARKET

STEP FIVE MARKETING OBJECTIVES AND STRATEGIES

STEP SIX POSITIONING STRATEGY

STEP SEVEN MARKETING MIX IMPLEMENTATION TOOLS

Product/Service
Branding
Packaging
Pricing
Distribution
Personal Selling/Operations

Promotion
Advertising Message
Advertising Media
Merchandising
Publicity

STEP EIGHT MARKETING PLAN BUDGET AND CALENDAR

STEP NINE EXECUTION

STEP TEN EVALUATION

Identifying Problems
and Opportunities

It is very difficult to develop a marketing plan without first consolidating and summarizing the objective material developed in the business review. The business review is a reference to be utilized throughout the year. It is meant to be exhaustive in the amount of data it presents and analyzes. However, in order to write a marketing plan, the marketer needs to crystallize specific company and product category challenges. The major conclusions from the business review should be polarized into problems to be solved and into opportunities to be exploited.

DEFINITION

Problems

Problems are derived from situations of weakness. As with opportunities, a problem statement can be drawn from a single finding or set of findings that make for a potentially negative situation. Reviewing the target market section in the business review for a retail client, we discovered that there was a heavy purchaser group, 30 percent of which purchased 65 percent of the product. The heaviest concentration was in the females age 35 to 49 with children group. Yet our client was strongest in attracting younger purchasers, and while the heavy purchaser shopped at our client's store for some products, the majority of her purchases were made elsewhere. This information led to the following problems under the Target Market heading:

- The company's purchaser tends to be younger, with fewer age 35 to 49 purchasers (the single strongest purchasing segment for heavy users) when compared to the heavy purchaser profile.

- The heavy purchaser is shopping our stores but making a majority of her purchases elsewhere.

Thus, to target the heavy user, the retailer had to develop a program to more fully satisfy the heavy purchaser's needs through the merchandise selection and do a better job of selling the customer on the full line of products.

In summary, problems focus on your firm's weaknesses. Problem statements also address market conditions that can result in a disadvantage for your company or the industry as a whole. The common denominator is that problems are defensive in nature. They will result in an action taken from a current position of weakness; you will be correcting a negative.

Opportunities

Opportunities are developed from strengths or positive circumstances. Often a combination of circumstances makes for a potentially positive situation, creating an opportunity. When we reviewed the competitive situation for a statewide accounting firm, we determined that there were very few accounting firms with aggressive, disciplined marketing programs. Even fewer actually advertised through mass communication vehicles. Also, we found that of the firms advertising, none was targeting small to medium sized businesses. An earlier demand analysis had shown that the greatest potential for our client was in providing a full range of accounting services to small to medium sized businesses in the retail, service, and financial SIC categories. This combination of information provided the following opportunities:

- While there is fairly heavy competition in the trading areas of the CPA firm, there is limited advertising of CPA services; no one CPA firm dominates either consumer or business awareness of accounting firms.

- No one firm is directly communicating to the small to medium sized business target market. Yet this market represents the majority of potential business in terms of actual numbers of clients.

These opportunities meant two things:

1. Because of the limited advertising clutter pertaining to accounting firms, an aggressive, targeted campaign could dominate the accounting advertising and build high awareness levels.

2. If the messages were strategic and thus meaningful to the target audience, then the increased share of mind or awareness level should be translated into increases in share of business or share of market.

In summary, opportunities are statements that point out strengths of the firm. They also identify areas where your company can exploit a weakness of the competition. They address market conditions that can result in an advantage to your company if positive action is taken. Opportunities are offensive in nature. They will result in an action capitalizing on strengths.

IDENTIFYING PROBLEMS AND OPPORTUNITIES

When writing your marketing plan, the marketing objectives and strategies come directly from the problems and opportunities. Ideally, each problem and opportunity should be addressed in the marketing plan. Therefore, make sure to develop problems and opportunities that are appropriate for each section of the business review.

First, make headings that correspond to the steps in your business review (e.g., Corporate Philosophy, Target Market, Sales Analysis, etc.). Leave plenty of room to summarize the problems and opportunities under each section heading (worksheets are provided at the end of this chapter). Next, review each section of the business review to identify as many meaningful problems and opportunities as possible. Make sure to review each section in the business review at least twice. Ask yourself, "Is this information actionable? Is it a current or potential problem that needs to be solved or an opportunity that can be exploited?"

Problem or Opportunity?

Many times what appears to be a problem can also be an opportunity. An example is the following sales analysis problem:

> While Heartland Men's Apparel sales are strong during the holiday period of November and December, sales are below that of the men's apparel category nationally. This situation occurs because Heartland Men's Apparel stores are not located in malls that generate heavy traffic during these periods.

While this is a problem for the company, it is also an opportunity. If national sales are at a peak during the November and December periods, then the opportunity exists to capture a larger percentage of these sales. However, because of the stores' locations, it is difficult to do as well as the average store nationally during this period. Thus, this statement is both a problem and an opportunity.

But the statement has to go somewhere. As a rule of thumb, try to determine if it is more of a problem or an opportunity. In this example, it is very difficult to change locations in retail, so this overriding factor would make the above statement a problem. In either case, however, the marketer would probably choose to address the problem or the opportunity by attempting to increase sales in the months of November and December.

HOW TO WRITE ACTIONABLE PROBLEMS AND OPPORTUNITIES

Problems and opportunities should be concise, one sentence statements that draw conclusions. This sentence would be underlined. If necessary, there can be a brief follow-up using supporting data or rationale. The rationale should utilize key factual data or findings from the business review. This will enable you to quickly support your problem and opportunity statements during a presentation.

The following are examples of problems and opportunities that demonstrate the writing style to use when formulating these statements. We selected one category of problems and one category of opportunities for examples. Remember that in your own problem and opportunity section, there will be problems and opportunities for each section of the business review.

Target Market Problems

- *Multiple target markets exist.* Each one has different demographics, needs, and wants. No single dominating customer group can be targeted.

- *The facial tissue's customers skew very old, with small to nonexistent percentage of users coming from teens and young adults.* The brand is developing virtually no new users from which to regenerate the consumer franchise.

- *General Hospital does not have a religious orientation.* The city of Johnsonville has a high concentration of Catholics (40 percent of the population). Of the two hospitals, the Catholic affiliated hospital dominates market share. Thus, religious factors influence the choice of hospital.

Purchase Rates/Buying Habits Opportunities

- *While the Southwest consumes more of the product on a per capita basis than any other part of the country, the Torger Company has relatively poor sales in this region.* This is because it has yet to fully expand distribution to this portion of the country.

- *The average shopper is extremely brand loyal.* Brand choice is developed at a young age with a majority of consumers continuing purchases for life.

- *Although total trial of the company's brands is very low, retrial is above the category average.* Thus, greater rates of consumers become regular users than is normal for the category, meaning product acceptance is very high.

Worksheet 3.1

Problems and Opportunities

Corporate Philosophy/Description of the Company

Problems

Opportunities

Target Market

Problems

Opportunities

Sales Analysis

Problems

Opportunities

Product Awareness and Attributes

Problems

Opportunities

Purchase Rates/Buying Habits

Problems

Opportunities

Distribution

Problems

Opportunities

Pricing

Problems

Opportunities

Historical Marketing Review of the Competition versus Your Company

Problems

Opportunities

Worksheet 3.1

Problems and Opportunities (Continued)

Demand Analysis

Problems

Opportunities

STEP THREE | Sales Objectives

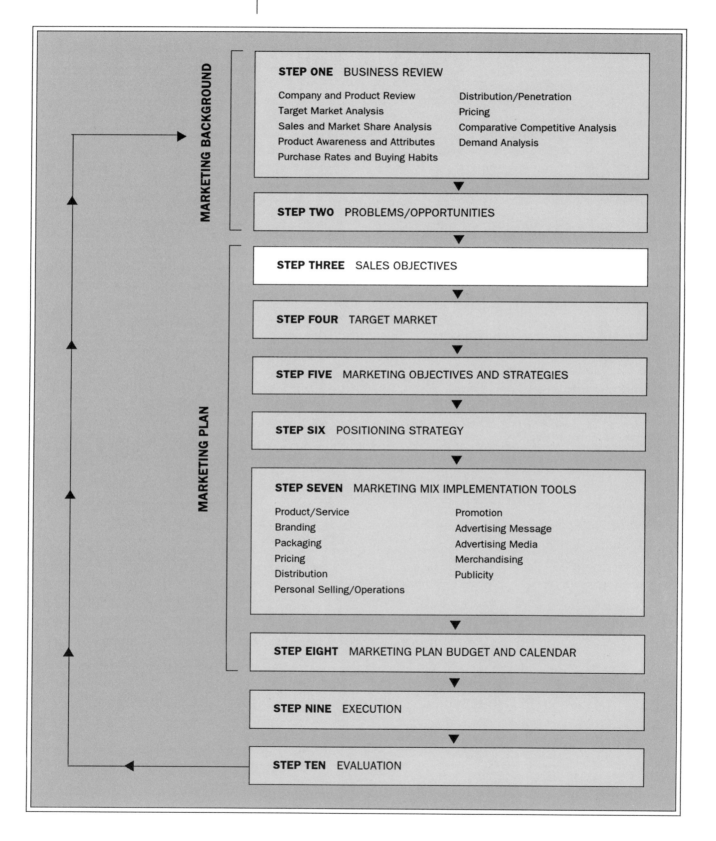

MARKETING BACKGROUND

STEP ONE BUSINESS REVIEW

Company and Product Review
Target Market Analysis
Sales and Market Share Analysis
Product Awareness and Attributes
Purchase Rates and Buying Habits

Distribution/Penetration
Pricing
Comparative Competitive Analysis
Demand Analysis

STEP TWO PROBLEMS/OPPORTUNITIES

MARKETING PLAN

STEP THREE SALES OBJECTIVES

STEP FOUR TARGET MARKET

STEP FIVE MARKETING OBJECTIVES AND STRATEGIES

STEP SIX POSITIONING STRATEGY

STEP SEVEN MARKETING MIX IMPLEMENTATION TOOLS

Product/Service
Branding
Packaging
Pricing
Distribution
Personal Selling/Operations

Promotion
Advertising Message
Advertising Media
Merchandising
Publicity

STEP EIGHT MARKETING PLAN BUDGET AND CALENDAR

STEP NINE EXECUTION

STEP TEN EVALUATION

Setting Sales Objectives

When you begin writing a marketing plan, the first task is setting sales objectives. This is one of the most complicated and important steps in preparing an effective marketing plan. The more you understand about the process of arriving at a sales objective, the easier it will be to write a marketing plan that will meet sales objectives.

DEFINITION

Sales objectives are projected levels of goods or services to be sold. Setting sales objectives is critical because it sets the tone of the marketing plan. Everything that follows in the plan is designed to meet the sales objectives—from defining the size of your target market and establishing marketing objectives, to determining the amount of advertising and promotion dollars to be budgeted, to the actual hiring of marketing and sales personnel, to the number and kinds of distribution channels/stores utilized, and, very importantly, to the amount of product produced or inventoried.

POINTS TO REMEMBER WHEN SETTING SALES OBJECTIVES

1. Because sales objectives have substantial impact on a business, they must be simultaneously challenging and attainable. Accordingly, sales objectives should be based on an accurate estimate of the market opportunity and the capacity of the organization to realize those opportunities.

2. You must set time specific sales objectives in order to provide a start and end date for your marketing program. It is also important to set both short-term and long-term sales objectives. Short-term sales objectives generally are for one year or less, while long-term ones usually include sales objectives for a minimum of three years.

3. Setting measurable sales objectives provides the means for determining what must be included in your marketing plan and for evaluating its success. Accordingly, sales objectives are quantified in terms of dollars and units for manufacturing firms, dollars and transactions (and occasionally units) for retail firms, and dollars and persons served for service firms.

4. Projected profits, a direct result of sales, should also be included in the sales objective section of your plan. Accordingly, as the author of this plan, you must understand the profit expectations to effectively prepare and evaluate the marketing plan. Further, if you are not operating in a pure business environment, keep in mind that sales objectives can be defined in terms other than dollars or units. As an example, for a nonprofit organization with programs dedicated to the prevention of child abuse, the goal might be a specific number of phone calls asking for help or reporting cases of abuse.

QUANTITATIVE AND QUALITATIVE FACTORS IN OBJECTIVE SETTING

Both quantitative and qualitative factors must be taken into consideration in the development of sales objectives. Quantitative factors are used first and can help to numerically calculate specific sales objectives, such as (1) the trending of the market and your company's share of the market, (2) sales history of your company, and (3) historical and projected company operating budgets along with profit expectations.

Qualitative factors are more subjective because of nonavailability and difficulty in quantifying certain types of information, such as the future economy and competition and where your product is relative to its life cycle. Therefore, interpretation of these additional subjective factors leads to an adjustment of the quantitatively based sales objectives.

HOW TO SET SALES OBJECTIVES

Worksheets for each step and a marketing plan format for writing the sales objectives are provided at the end of this chapter.

The methodology of setting sales objectives incorporates both quantitative and qualitative factors, which means your sales objectives will be a composite of data based estimates and educated guesses.

The Process of Setting Sales Objectives

The recommended process to set your sales objectives is based on three steps:

- Set individual sales objectives using three different quantitative methods.

- Reconcile these different quantitative goals into composite sales objectives.

- Adjust the quantitatively arrived at composite sales objectives through the interpolation of the relevant subjective qualitative factors, such as the economy and competition.

Step 1 : Set Quantitative Sales Objectives

If the data are available, we suggest that you use three different quantitative methods: outside macro, inside micro, and expense plus. Each method will develop a sales objective estimate, and each estimate will provide one of three parameters from which to make realistic judgments in arriving at final sales objectives. Each method can be used exclusively in arriving at a sales objective; however, the final outcome will not be as reliable as when you apply all three approaches. By using the three different approaches, you develop sales objectives derived from three different sets of data—a safeguard against using only one set of data that might not be totally reliable or encompassing.

Outside Macro Approach. In this approach, first look outside of your immediate company environment and estimate *total market or category sales* for each of the *next three years*. Follow this with an estimate of your company's share of the market for the next three years. Then multiply the total market or category projections by the market share estimate for each of the next years to arrive at your sales objectives. You should end up with a three-year projection for both unit and dollar sales.

To arrive at these estimates, begin with a review of the past five-year trend of each marketplace in which your product, service, or retail store competes. (If you don't have five years of sales data available, use what data you have, and supplement it with available data from similar businesses to arrive at a trending of the marketplace.) If the market is trending up at a 5 percent rate, you could project the market to continue to grow at this rate for each of the next three years.

Market Trend Line Sales Projection. Other than applying a straight percentage increase to arrive at market volume for future years, you can statistically develop a market trend line. If you were projecting sales in dollars for 1996 and you had a market change from $800,000 in 1988 to $900,000 in 1993, you would do the following:

Market change 1988 to 1993 = $100,000
($800,000 to $900,000)

Market change period = 5 years
(1988 to 1993)

Average $ change per year = $20,000
($100,000/5)

$ change for 8-year period (1988 to 1996) = $160,000
($20,000 x 8)

Projected $ sales for 1996 = $960,000
($800,000 from base year 1988 + $160,000 for change over 8-year period)

This method of projecting sales is referred to as *freehand,* and it is the simplest method of determining trend lines. You can use this trend line approach for both dollars and unit sales. If there is a substantial fluctuation in past sales year by year, you can arrive at a mathematically generated trend line by the least squares method. If this is necessary, we suggest you refer to a text on business statistics.

Company/Product Trend Line Share Projection. To arrive at a share of market estimate, review the change in your company's share over the past five years and project a similar share change for the future. You can estimate a percentage point change or use the freehand approach. If you were estimating a share number for 1994, and your share changed from 10 percent in 1988 to 16.5 percent in 1993, you would do the following:

Share change 1988 to 1993 = 6.5 points
(from 10 percent to 16.5 percent)

Share change period = 5 years
(1988 to 1993)

Average change per year = 1.3 points
(6.5 points/5 years)

Share change for 6-year period (1988 to 1994) = 7.8 points
(1.3 x 6)

Projected share for 1994 = 17.8 percent
(10 percent share from base year 1988 + 7.8 percentage
point change over 6-year period)

Again, once you have arrived at a projected number for market sales and units and a projected share of the market for each, multiply the total market estimates by the estimated market shares to arrive at a sales objective for dollars and units. You would apply this macro method in each of the years you are developing sales objectives. Exhibit 4.1 provides an example of how this method can be used. Modify the worksheet at the end of this chapter to include transactions if you are in the retail business, or from units to persons/companies served if you are in the service business.

Inside Micro Approach. Having reviewed the broad macro outside market sales, next review your own organization's sales history. Start at the *top* or with a review of your organization's total sales. Using the straight percentage increase or the trend line approach, arrive at projected three-year sales for your company. From the top go further and, using the straight percentage or trend line approach, estimate sales for each product or department, adding the projected sales of each product or department together for a three-year company total. Then reconcile this pieced together total with your initial sales estimate for the entire organization for an ultimate top projection.

Next, review your sales by dollars and units from the *bottom up* to arrive at an estimated sales figure. Bottom up means estimating sales from where they are generated, such as sales by each channel, store unit, or service office/center. Based on history and changes in the marketplace, estimate sales for each bottom up sales generator, and add them together for each year's projection. You can use the straight percentage change or trend line approach for each year's projection. However, because of the vast amount or lack of data to process, you might have to estimate rather than calculate each sales

EXHIBIT 4.1 Sales Objectives: Macro Method

Market and Share Data

	Market Sales Volume				Company Share Percent of the Market			
	$ (MM)	Percent Change Previous Year	Units (MM)	Percent Change Previous Year	$	Percent Points Change from Previous Year	Units	Percent Points Change from Previous Year
Previous 5 Years								
1989	$ 952.2	13.3%	449.1	5.1%	5.0%	0.1	4.0%	0.2
1990	1,067.0	12.1	484.0	7.8	5.1	0.1	4.7	0.7
1991	1,135.1	6.4	508.2	5.0	6.1	1.0	5.2	0.5
1992	1,202.9	6.0	527.9	3.9	6.5	0.4	5.7	0.5
1993	1,275.0	6.0	544.0	3.0	6.6	0.1	6.1	0.4
Projections Next 3 years								
1994	1,355.7	6.3	567.7	4.4	7.0	0.4	6.6	0.5
1995	1,436.4	5.9	591.4	4.1	7.4	0.4	7.1	0.5
1996	1,517.1	5.6	615.1	4.0	7.8	0.4	7.6	0.5

Three-Year Sales Projection for Company

	Dollars				Units		
Year	Market Sales Volume (MM)	X Company Share Percent of Market	= Company Sales (MM)	Market Sales Unit Volume (MM)	X Company Unit Share Percent of Market	= Company Unit Sales (MM)
1994	$ 1,355.7	7.0%	$ 94.9	567.7	6.6%	37.5
1995	1,436.4	7.4	106.3	591.4	7.1	42.0
1996	1,517.1	7.8	118.3	615.1	7.6	47.0

projection. Make sure, for either approach used, that you factor in anticipated price increases for your company products for the bottom up and top projections. Exhibit 4.2 provides an example of how to prepare a top to bottom sales forecast.

If you are in a manufacturing business, your bottom up generator becomes the distribution channel (e.g., direct accounts, wholesaler/distributors, etc.). If you are in a retail business, estimate by store, by market, by district/region, building up to a total sales estimate. Use this same building approach if you are in a service business. It is often a good idea to have participation by the sales force or the retail/service people in the field, who estimate sales by their area of responsibility. To arrive at a final micro sales objective, you must then reconcile the organization's sales estimates derived from the top with those derived from the bottom.

Expense Plus Approach. Once you have the outside macro based estimates and the inside micro based estimates, it makes good sense to estimate the sales level needed to cover planned expenses and make a profit. This budget based sales objective approach is more short term in nature and is most useful in helping to arrive at your one-year sales objective. A sales objective arrived at from expense and profit

EXHIBIT 4.2   Sales Objectives: Micro Method

Projection from Top: Sales Forecast for Manufacturing, Service, or Retail Category*

	Company Sales Volume			
	$ (MM)	Percent Change Previous Year	Units (MM)	Percent Change Previous Year
Previous 5 Years				
1989	$ 47.7	10.3%	20.2	6.0%
1990	54.1	13.4	22.8	12.8
1991	68.8	27.1	28.8	26.3
1992	78.0	13.3	32.7	13.5
1993	84.2	7.9	34.0	4.0
Projections Next 3 Years				
1994	93.3	10.8	37.5	10.3
1995	102.4	9.8	41.0	9.3
1996	111.5	8.9	44.4	8.3

Projections from Bottom: Sales Forecast by Distribution Channel for Manufacturers*†

	Existing			New		
	Number	Dollars (MM)	Units	Number	Dollars (MM)	Units
Direct accounts	25	$ 29.2	9.2	6	$ 5.6	2.4
Wholesalers/Brokers	74	62.4	26.5	6	2.1	0.9
Other	—	—	—	—	—	—
Total	99	$ 91.6	35.7	12	$ 7.7	3.3

Projections from Bottom: Sales Forecast by Store for Retailers*†

Market	Existing Stores	
	Dollars (000)	Transactions (000)
Green Bay/Store Number		
3	$ 773.7	73.6
4	276.8	25.2
5	449.8	41.8
7	285.6	23.2
8	343.5	30.5
Market Total	$ 2,129.4	194.3
Madison/Store Number		
1	$ 644.1	59.5
2	396.6	35.0
6	534.7	46.0
9 (new, open 9 months)	400.0	36.0
Market Total	$ 1,975.4	176.5
Grand Total	$ 4,104.8	370.8

* Based on your type of business, include in your sales projections dollars and units/ transactions/persons served, and take into consideration *new* products, distribution channels, stores or services, and price changes. Service organizations use service office/center in place of stores. Manufacturers use net dollars sales to trade/ intermediate markets and retail/service firms use dollar sales to ultimate purchasers.

† For bottom up projections, develop projections for each year for a three-year period.

expectations can differ dramatically from a sales objective generated from a market or company sales trend projection. This difference in projections may signal the need for a more conservative or aggressive marketing plan. Although very simplistic, it is also very real, because it details the sales that have to be generated to stay in business and make a profit.

To arrive at a sales objective using this method, you will need budget data. If your company has been doing business for a number of years, it is relatively easy to estimate expenses and expected profits for the next year by reviewing your historical business data. It is a good learning experience, particularly if you are new in the business, to review the cost of goods, operating margins, expenses, and profits within the industry and for other comparable businesses. Industry guidelines such as this are available from libraries, trade associations, and the business census.

A number of methods can be used to develop a budget based sales objective. Using a common approach we apply in our business, called expense plus, you first estimate your operating expenses (marketing, administrative, etc.) in total dollars for the upcoming year. Next, from your expected gross margin percentage, subtract your expected profit percentage (before taxes) to provide an estimated expense percentage. Expected gross margin is determined by dividing anticipated net sales by gross sales; net sales is determined by subtracting cost of goods sold from gross sales. The gross margin percentage or the data needed from its determination is available from both historical company records and/or from industry guideline data. The estimated expense percentage is divided into the estimated expense dollars to determine the required sales necessary to meet expense and profit goals. Exhibit 4.3 presents an example of a review of data and calculations for the expense plus approach.

Step 2: Reconcile Sales Objectives

Now that you have arrived at outside macro sales objectives, inside micro sales objectives, and an expense plus sales objective, you must reconcile the differences to establish the sales objectives for your marketing plan. This

EXHIBIT 4.3   Sales Objectives: Expense Plus Method (Budget Based for One Year)

Previous 5 Years	Gross Margin Percent of Sales	Profit Percent of Sales	Expenses	
			Percent of Sales	Dollars (MM)
1989	33.4%	4.5%	29.1%	$ 13.9
1990	35.1	3.1	32.1	17.1
1991	37.2	3.1	34.1	23.5
1992	35.2	1.0	35.5	27.7
1993	31.3	1.0	30.1	28.0

Expected Margin 33.5% – Expected Profit 3.5% = Operating Expense 30.0%

Budgeted Expense Dollars $28.5 (MM)/Operating Expense 30.0% = Sales Objective $95.0 (MM)

EXHIBIT 4.4 Method for Reconciling Sales Objectives

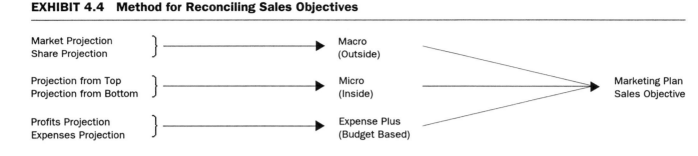

EXHIBIT 4.5 Reconciliation of Sales Objectives

	Macro		Micro		Expense Plus	Composite Sales Objectives	
	Dollars (MM)	Units (MM)	Dollars (MM)	Units (MM)	Dollars (MM)	Dollars (MM)	Units (MM)
Short Term							
1994	$ 94.9	37.5	$ 96.3	38.2	$ 95.0	$ 95.4	37.9
Long Term							
1995	106.3	42.0	103.4	40.1		104.9	41.1
1996	118.3	47.0	112.2	45.1		115.3	46.1

methodology is shown in Exhibit 4.4. After reviewing your sales objective alternatives based on this methodology, you may decide to go with a pure average of the three or a weighted average, placing more emphasis on one alternative than the other. Or you may use the (weighted) average of two, or just one. The important aspect of Step 2 is that you have reviewed the data from various quantitative perspectives. This will help you arrive at a sales objective with your eyes wide open and with an understanding of the dynamics of setting a sales objective. For the most meaningful sales projections, attempt to apply all three methods, or at the very minimum, two methods that you can use for comparison. Exhibit 4.5 shows how reconciliation of the three methods' goals into a composite sales objective can be accomplished. A worksheet is provided at the end of this chapter.

Step 3: Qualitative Adjustment of Quantitative Sales

Now that you have arrived at quantitative sales objectives, you should review again the qualitative factors that will have an impact on future sales. You need to temper the numerically derived sales objectives with the more qualitative forecasting factors. Using the appropriate qualitative factors, you can increase or decrease the composite dollars and unit/transactions/persons served sales objectives through an assignment of positive or negative percentage points depending on the estimated degree of impact by each qualitative

EXHIBIT 4.6   Qualitative Adjustment of Quantitative Factors

Qualitative Impacting Factors	Point Change	Percentage Adjustment	X	Composite Sales Objective (MM)	=	Adjusted Sales Objective (MM)
1. Economy	+ 2	1.02		$ 95.4		$ 97.3
2. Competition	– 4	.96		95.4		91.6
				Total		$ 188.9
				Final Adjusted Average (Total of adjusted sales objectives divided by number of calculated factors)		$ 94.5

Note: 1. List qualitative factors and to what extent they will impact on the previously arrived at numerical sales objectives.

     Adjust composite sales objective(s) accordingly to arrive at final sales objective(s).

   2. Use qualitative adjustments for units, transactions, or persons served, as well as for sales dollars objectives.

     However, percentage point adjustment may differ from dollars.

factor. If the economy is growing and the economic outlook is bright, you might increase the composite sales objective by two percentage points. Or you may decrease the composite sales objective by four percentage points because an aggressive competitor moved into your trading area. If there is more than one major impacting factor, you can balance their effect through averaging. Exhibit 4.6 illustrates how you would calculate these factors.

Plan to Revise the Sales Objectives

The sales objectives will most likely be revised more than once as you write the marketing plan. You may uncover greater than expected sales potential among a target market. Or you may determine that your company does not have the necessary capital, there is greater competition than expected, or there is not enough consumer demand, which could all negatively affect the estimated sales objectives.

Once your marketing plan is finalized (ideally, two or three months before the start of your fiscal year), it is wise to keep your sales objectives current. Review your sales objectives at two months, five months, and eight months into the marketing plan year in order to adjust the sales objectives for the second, third, and fourth quarters of your fiscal year. This will help you maximize your sales and control your expenses in a timely and profitable manner.

Worksheet 4.1   Sales Objectives: Macro Method

Market and Share Data

	Market Sales Volume				Company Share Percent of the Market			
	$ ( )	Percent Change Previous Year	Units ( )	Percent Change Previous Year	$	Percent Points Change from Previous Year	Units	Percent Points Change from Previous Year

Previous 5 Years
1
2
3
4
5

Projections Next 3 Years
1
2
3

Three-Year Sales Projection for Company

	Dollars				Units			
Year	Market Sales $ Volume ( )	X	Company Share Percent of Market	Company $ Sales = ( )	Market Sales Unit Volume ( )	X	Company Unit Share Percent of Market	Company Unit Sales = ( )
1								
2								
3								

Worksheet 4.2   Sales Objectives: Micro Method

Projection from Top: Sales Forecast for Manufacturing, Service, or Retail Category*

	Company Sales Volume			
	$ ( )	Percent Change Previous Year	Units ( )	Percent Change Previous Year
Previous 5 Years				
1				
2				
3				
4				
5				
Projections Next 3 Years				
1				
2				
3				

Note: Complete a worksheet for your company's total sales and a worksheet for each individual product or department.

* Based on your type of business, include in your sales projections dollars and units/transactions/persons served, and take into consideration *new* products, distribution channels, stores or services, and price changes. Use net dollar sales to trade/intermediate markets.

Projections from Bottom: Sales Forecast by Distribution Channel for Manufacturers*

	Existing			New		
	Number	Dollars (MM)	Units	Number	Dollars (MM)	Units
Direct accounts		$			$	
Wholesalers/Brokers						
Other						
Total						

Note: Develop projections for each year for a three-year period.

* In your sales projections, take into consideration *new* products, changes in distribution outlets, and price changes. Use net dollar sales to trade/intermediate markets.

Projections from Bottom: Sales Forecast by Store for Retailers*

	Stores	
Market	$ ( )	Transactions ( )
Name/Store number		
Market total		

Note: Develop projections for each year for a three-year period.

* In your sales projections, take into consideration *new* stores, products, and services along with price changes. Service organizations use service office/center in place of stores. Use dollar sales to ultimate purchasers. Service organizations use persons served in place of transactions.

Worksheet 4.3

Sales Objectives: Expense Plus Method (Budget Based for One Year)
(Historical Review and Calculation)

Budget Based for One Year

Previous 5 Years	Gross Margin Percent of Sales	Profit Percent of Sales	Expenses	
			Percent of Sales	Dollars ( )
1				
2				
3				
4				
5				

Expected Margin _____ % – Expected Profit _____ % = Operating Expense _____ %.

Budget Expense Dollars $ _____ /Operating Expense _____ % = Sales Objective $ _____ .

Worksheet 4.4   Sales Objectives

Reconciliation of Sales Objectives

	Macro		Micro		Expense Plus			Composite Sales Objectives	
	$	Units	$	Units	$	$			Units
	( )	( )	( )	( )	( )	( )			( )

Short-Term
1-year

Long-Term
2-year
3-year

Worksheet 4.5   Qualitative Adjustment of Quantitative Factors

Qualitative Impacting Factors	+/– Point Change	Percentage Adjustment	X	Composite Sales Objective	=	Adjusted Sales Objective
				Total		
				Final Adjusted Average		_____
				(Total of adjusted sales objectives divided by number of calculated factors)		

Note: 1. List qualitative factors and to what extent they will impact on the previously arrived at numerical sales objectives.
　　　　Adjust composite sales objective(s) accordingly to arrive at final sales objective(s).
　　2. Use qualitative adjustments for units, transactions, or persons served, as well as for sales dollars objectives.
　　　　However, percentage point adjustment may differ from dollars.

Worksheet 4.6   Sales Objective Formats for Manufacturers

Short-Term (One-Year)

1. Increase dollar sales _____ % over previous year, from $ _____ to $ _____ .

2. Increase unit sales _____ % over previous year, from _____ to _____ .

Long-Term*

1. Increase dollar sales _____ % from 19 _____ to 19 _____ , from $ _____ to $ _____ .

2. Increase unit sales _____ % from 19 _____ to 19 _____ , from _____ to _____ .

Rationale

Note: 1. Use this format for total company sales as well as for specific products.
　　2. Include profit objectives as well, using a similar format.

*List two- and three-year sales objectives separately.

Worksheet 4.7   Sales Objective Formats for Retail and Service*

Short-Term (One-Year)

1. Increase total sales _____ % and transactions _____ % over previous year, from $ _____ to $ _____

   and from _____ transactions to _____ transactions.

2. Increase comparable store sales _____ % and transactions _____ % over previous year, from $_____

   to $ _____ and from _____ transactions to _____ transactions.

Long-Term†

1. Increase total sales _____ % and transactions _____ % for 19 _____ to 19 _____ ,

   from $ _____ to $ _____ and from _____ transactions to _____ transactions.

2. Increase comparable store sales _____ % and transactions _____ % for 19 _____ to 19 _____ ,

   from $ _____ to $ _____ and from _____ transactions to _____ transactions.

Rationale

Note: 1. Use this format for total company sales as well as for specific retail and service categories. Retailers might also want to use unit objectives as well.
      Service organizations use dollar and persons/companies served.
   2. Include profit objectives as well using a similar format.

†List two- and three-year sales objectives separately.

STEP FOUR | Target Market

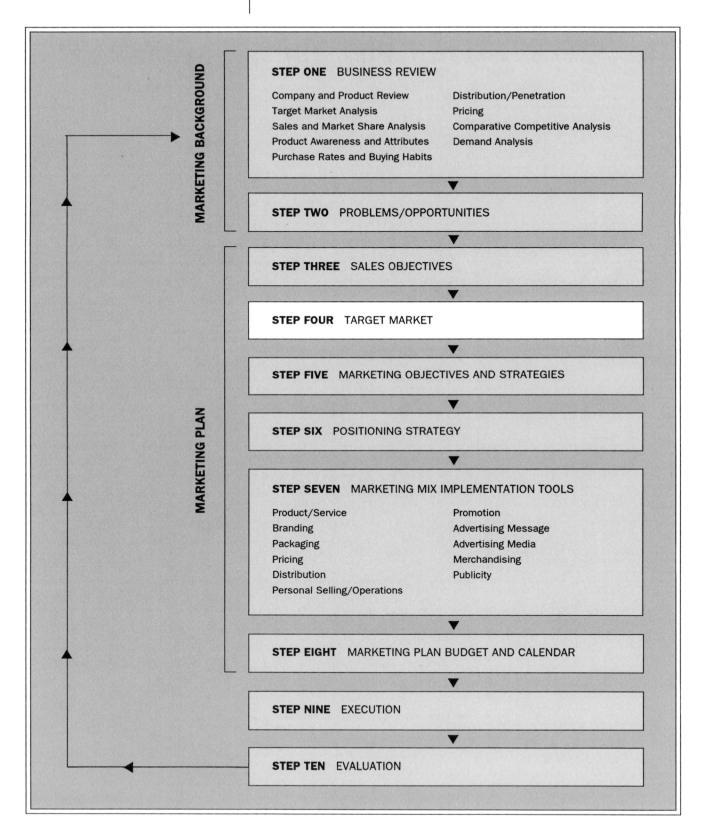

MARKETING BACKGROUND

STEP ONE BUSINESS REVIEW

Company and Product Review
Target Market Analysis
Sales and Market Share Analysis
Product Awareness and Attributes
Purchase Rates and Buying Habits

Distribution/Penetration
Pricing
Comparative Competitive Analysis
Demand Analysis

STEP TWO PROBLEMS/OPPORTUNITIES

MARKETING PLAN

STEP THREE SALES OBJECTIVES

STEP FOUR TARGET MARKET

STEP FIVE MARKETING OBJECTIVES AND STRATEGIES

STEP SIX POSITIONING STRATEGY

STEP SEVEN MARKETING MIX IMPLEMENTATION TOOLS

Product/Service
Branding
Packaging
Pricing
Distribution
Personal Selling/Operations

Promotion
Advertising Message
Advertising Media
Merchandising
Publicity

STEP EIGHT MARKETING PLAN BUDGET AND CALENDAR

STEP NINE EXECUTION

STEP TEN EVALUATION

Defining the Target Market

While a company's profits are derived from sales, sales are totally dependent on the purchasers and users of your product. Because it is the reason for your product's existence and the key to finding the marketing answers, let your target market drive your marketing plan.

DEFINITION

Once you have developed sales objectives, you must determine to whom you will be selling your product. Making this determination is really defining a target market—a group of people with a set of common characteristics. Target marketing allows for a concentration of effort against a portion of the population with similar purchasing needs and buying habits.

Segmentation is a selection process that divides the broad consuming market into manageable segments with common characteristics, enabling you to realize the greatest potential sales at the lowest cost. Develop your target market by first selecting the current and potential purchaser and/or user of your product and, second, by breaking down this broad group into the most relevant segments for the most effective and efficient communication and selling of your product.

In segmenting your target markets, you define the ultimate purchasers or users of your product, who will become your *primary target.* You also may find it necessary to define and consider *secondary targets,* such as a smaller but growing or high consuming and/or very profitable segment. Other potential secondary targets might be influencer markets. If you are marketing a consumer service of a hospital, you would market not only to potential patients but also to the physicians who, as influencers, refer patients to the hospital.

CONSUMER PRIMARY TARGET MARKET

Step 1: Determine Purchaser and/or User

You must determine whether the primary target group will include purchasers, users, or both. However, keep in mind that it is very difficult to effectively market to two primary markets. Because this is the first and most encompassing step in the defining process, step back and attempt to determine which of these two targets is the driving force and what makes up their purchase and usage behavior. Consider these five factors in your determination:

- The amount purchased and/or used
- The degree of influence on the usage and purchase decision
- The size of the market
- Who the competition chooses as its target market
- The inherent benefits of your product to one target or the other

If the user and the purchaser are different, whom do you make the primary target for your marketing efforts: the user or the purchaser? Or do you target both? If you do not dominate the market in terms of sales and marketing dollars (as is most often the case), concentrate your marketing efforts against one target market rather than fragmenting your efforts over many and making minimal impact.

Once you have made your user/purchaser target market decision, make sure your primary target can be defined by a unified profile of similarities, from demographics and geography to consumer benefits and purchasing behavior. For a retailer marketing fabric to sewers (the purchaser is usually the user as well), product attributes or benefits became the primary means of defining the target market. Because not all sewers consider both large selection and low prices of fabrics equally important in choosing one fabric store over the other, the retailer made women age 25 to 54 *interested in fabric selection* its primary target, because it could not profitably deliver the price benefit as well as selection.

Step 2: Compare Current Target to the Demographic and Geographic Market Profile

Now that you have determined the primary user or purchaser, compare the demographic profile of the category to the demographic profile of your current customers, which you can quantify through market and/or customer research. By comparing your customer market with the demographics of the total category, you can determine whether you must adjust your current target focus to realize greater market potential for your product. Through an analysis for a retail client experiencing low sales per store, we found that its customer target market was primarily blue-collar with an annual income of under $30,000, while the majority of purchasers in the total category were white-collar with annual incomes over $30,000, skewing to $40,000.

Based on your findings, you may want to alter your initial target market profile description to more closely mirror the product category's target market in order to expand your current customer base. Or this exercise may simply point out the major differences between consumers of your company's product and those of the category and provide insight about why your company is successfully capturing a specific segment of the product category and how to attract even more of the same consumers.

Further, based on your business review, you should have determined regions, markets, and/or areas of markets that have the greatest consumption potential for your product by comparing the overall category usage of your product by area relative to the sales of your product. Based on this analysis, you may want to expand, reduce, or merely refine the geographic focus of your target market. This geographic comparison can be used for an individual store or retail trading area and specific markets, as well as for a region of the country.

A word of caution: Before you go on to develop a new market or modify an existing target, make sure you have profitably exploited the full potential of your current customer base. This is particularly true in retail, service, and business-to-business marketing where you have personal contact with your customers. Your own customers in most cases are your most important and potentially profitable target market, because they are responsible for your firm's current existence and are a prime target for future sales. Target your current customers not only to retain their purchase loyalty, but also to motivate them to make more and bigger purchases and to refer new customers.

Step 3: Determine Whether There Is a Heavy User or Purchaser Target

Having decided on the broad user versus purchaser market along with a demographic and geographic target, a final step is to analyze the target market data in Steps 2 or 3 of your business review to determine whether there is a heavy user for your product. As a guideline, you have a heavy user in your product category if approximately two-thirds or more of total product is consumed by approximately one-third or fewer of the total users. A few percentage points below 67 percent of total usage and a few points above 33 percent of users is acceptable. For example, 35 percent of canned vegetable users consume 65 percent of canned vegetables.

With a *one-third user to two-thirds consumption* determination, this heavy user usually becomes your primary target, and you define it based on descriptive data available to you. For the consumer market, the heavy user description could include demography, geography, and possibly lifestyle and product benefit/usage information, if available.

BUSINESS-TO-BUSINESS PRIMARY TARGET MARKET

Step 1: Define Your Existing Core Customers

Through your target market analysis in Step 3 of the business review, you should have a clear understanding of your current customer companies in terms of Standard Industrial Classification (SIC), size, geography, application of your product, organizational structure, and new versus repeat usage. You must decide whether to focus your marketing efforts on selling more to your key primary customers or selling more products to lesser purchasing customers who have high purchasing potential. What is most efficient? What holds more short-term and long-term potential?

Make sure you segment your current customer base into heavy and light users of your product to determine where you should focus your marketing energies and dollars. In working with one of our clients who manufactures craft supplies, we discovered that, although they were spending nearly half their time and marketing dollars selling directly to craft retailers, over 80 percent of their sales were being made directly to distributors. Further analysis showed that 10 out of 400 distributors to whom they were marketing accounted for nearly 40 percent of distributor sales and 33 percent of total sales. The result of refocusing the primary emphasis on these core customers meant more efficient use of available marketing resources and greater sales, along with insight into the need to find and sell to similar companies.

Step 2: Target High Potential New Customers

After redefining your current customer target market to fully exploit its buying potential, next compare your target customer to the marketplace (national and state SIC charts in the business review), selecting those customer SIC categories with the greatest potential.

New Potential Customers within SIC Categories Where Your Company Does Business

Within each SIC category where your company does business, target companies that best match your high volume customers in terms of size (sales dollars, number of employees, number of outlets if retail) and geography, not neglecting application of product and organization structure (one location versus branches). You can select these potential companies from the individual state industrial directories (available from state governments) that provide a complete listing of in-state commercial and industrial firms.

Potential Customers in SIC Categories Where Your Company Does Not Do Business

Also, do not neglect the SIC categories in which your company has no or minimal market share, if you sell a product or service that would fulfill the needs of companies in those categories. In working with a statewide CPA firm that was strong in serving the accounting needs of companies in the financial field, we found it was also very effective to market their services to retailers, even though this CPA firm originally had only a small share of this category.

Step 3: Define the Decision Makers and the Decision Making Process

Once you have segmented the customer and noncustomer companies, you must target the specific decision makers, as well as determine their function and influence in the decision process. Further, you must determine the decision sequence and the purchase criteria. Which decision maker does the initial screening of your product? Who makes the final decision? Is the decision maker looking for the very best quality product and then the best price, or vice versa? Is service most important? Many times you cannot answer these questions unless you first define who the real decision maker is and if there is more than one.

SECONDARY
TARGET MARKETS

Now that you have made a primary target market determination, it is wise to consider secondary targets that you originally discarded because they did not account for the majority of sales volume or sales potential.

Consumer Secondary Targets

In the process of determining your primary consumer market, you most likely discovered target markets that have heavy concentration of usage but that do not account for a high percentage of total volume. In this case, you could make these concentration segments secondary targets and place additional emphasis on them. As a result, you might develop special promotion programs and add selective media weight for the secondary target. Examples of these secondary targets would be the Hispanic market's heavy usage of flour for meal preparation; college students' heavy beer usage; and salesmen as frequent suit purchasers.

Also affecting purchase or usage is the *influencer,* who most often becomes a secondary target. Through primary research for a retail men's apparel chain, we found that wives influence the suit and sport coat purchases of their husbands in over 50 percent of all purchase decisions. So in this situation, the male who is the purchaser and user should be the primary target, but his wife cannot be totally ignored and thus becomes a secondary target.

Business-to-Business Secondary Targets

In business-to-business situations, a secondary target will often be a customer who does not purchase heavily from your company currently but has high purchasing potential. You can delineate the potential of this customer by estimating your competitors' sales to this customer and determining what additional needs your company can fulfill for this customer.

HOW TO WRITE
TARGET MARKET
DESCRIPTORS

Once you have arrived at your final target markets, you can use the worksheets at the end of this chapter to list them. Exhibits 5.1 and 5.2 illustrate the format for writing target market descriptors for a consumer and business-to-business firm.

EXHIBIT 5.1 Target Market for a Retail Casual Apparel Chain

Primary Target Market

Value conscious purchasers of casual apparel for the family:

  Married women
  Age 18 to 49
  Household size 3+
  Household income $25M +
  Employed
  Reside in size B and C counties
  High school education

Secondary Target Market

Purchasers of durable, value oriented casual/work apparel for self:

  Men 18 to 49
  Income $25M +
  Reside in size B and C counties
  Better education than women's apparel purchasers

EXHIBIT 5.2 Target Market for a Manufacturer of Computer Form Paper

Primary Target Market

Firms that purchase customized stock form computer paper:

Current Customers
Companies
  SIC: 20 to 39 (Manufacturing), 60 to 70 (Finance, Insurance, and Real Estate)
  Size: 25,000 cases or more purchased per year per company
  Geography: East Central and West Central regions
Decision Makers
  Data processing managers
  Purchasing agents

Secondary Target Market

Firms that purchase customized stock form computer paper:

Prospects
Companies
  SIC: 20 to 39 (Manufacturing), 60 to 67 (Finance, Insurance, and Real Estate), 70-99
    (Business Services)
  Size: Minimum 1,000 cases or more purchased per year
  Geography: East Central, West Central, and Atlantic Seaboard regions
Decision Makers
  Data processing managers
  Purchasing agents

Worksheet 5.1   Target Market for Consumer (Packaged Goods, Retail, Service)

Primary Market

Secondary Market (Where Applicable)

Users/Purchasers

Influencers

Rationale

Worksheet 5.2   **Target Market for Business-to-Business**

Primary*

Secondary* (Where Applicable)

Intermediate

End User

Other

Rationale

---

*List decision makers with descriptor whenever possible.

STEP FIVE | Marketing Objectives and Strategies

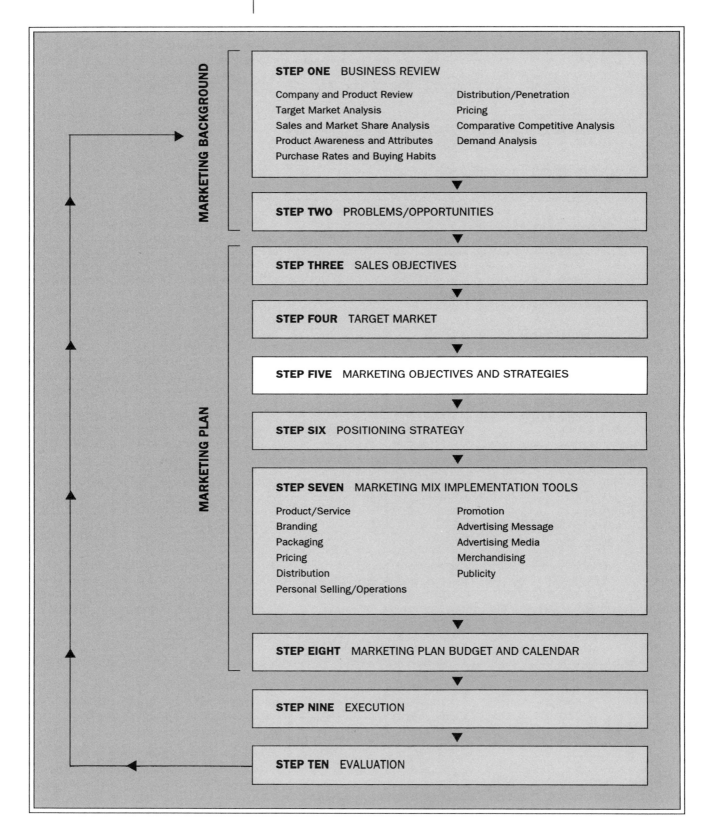

MARKETING BACKGROUND

STEP ONE BUSINESS REVIEW

Company and Product Review
Target Market Analysis
Sales and Market Share Analysis
Product Awareness and Attributes
Purchase Rates and Buying Habits

Distribution/Penetration
Pricing
Comparative Competitive Analysis
Demand Analysis

STEP TWO PROBLEMS/OPPORTUNITIES

MARKETING PLAN

STEP THREE SALES OBJECTIVES

STEP FOUR TARGET MARKET

STEP FIVE MARKETING OBJECTIVES AND STRATEGIES

STEP SIX POSITIONING STRATEGY

STEP SEVEN MARKETING MIX IMPLEMENTATION TOOLS

Product/Service
Branding
Packaging
Pricing
Distribution
Personal Selling/Operations

Promotion
Advertising Message
Advertising Media
Merchandising
Publicity

STEP EIGHT MARKETING PLAN BUDGET AND CALENDAR

STEP NINE EXECUTION

STEP TEN EVALUATION

6

Setting Marketing Objectives and Strategies

Marketing objectives and strategies form the foundation of the marketing plan. Marketing objectives describe *what* needs to be achieved in order to meet the sales goals, and marketing strategies describe *how* the objectives will be accomplished.

<table>
<tr>
<td>

MARKETING OBJECTIVES

</td>
<td>

Definition

A *marketing objective* is a statement of what needs to be accomplished. Marketing objectives are ends to be achieved. Differentiating between marketing objectives and marketing strategies is not always easy and is a source of confusion even for experienced marketing professionals. To show the difference between the two, we have detailed those properties we believe make up a marketing objective. A marketing objective must:

- *Be specific.* The objective should focus on one singular goal.

- *Be measurable.* The results must be able to be quantified.

- *Relate to a specific time period.* This can be one or more years, the next six months, or even specific months of the year.

- *Focus on affecting target market behavior.* (For example, encouraging shopping, trial of a product, repeat purchase of a product, larger purchases, more frequent purchases, etc.) Often, objectives are set for individual segments of the target market.

Current and Potential New Users

Marketing objectives relate to target markets and focus on influencing their behavior. Marketing objectives will therefore fall into one of two target market categories: current users or new users (this could also apply to purchasers). Within each category there are two major objectives to be achieved. Keep in mind that most, though not all, marketing plans develop marketing objectives for both current and new users—thus there are multiple marketing objectives.

</td>
</tr>
</table>

Current Users

Retention of Current Users. A common marketing objective is to retain the customer base at its current size from both a number and a dollar standpoint. This objective is defensive in nature. If your company has been losing customers over the past year or two, it becomes necessary to reverse this trend and maintain your customer base. You need to direct total focus first toward determining why business has been lost, and then toward stabilizing the customer base.

Increased Purchases from Current Users. If your customer base is already stable, the objective can take a more offensive direction with strategies designed to obtain additional business from existing customers. This can be accomplished three different ways—by getting your customers to purchase more often or more times in a given month or year, a more expensive product or service, or greater volume or amounts of product during each purchase.

Potential New Users

Increase Trial of Your Product or Service. For retailers, this equates to first getting increased traffic into the store. Most retailers have a fairly consistent purchase ratio (percentage of times a consumer purchases versus leaves without purchasing), which means that the retailer can rely on a certain percentage of the increased traffic actually making a purchase.

Increased trial for package goods, service, and business-to-business firms equates to *actual use of the product.* However, in both the retail situation and in package goods, service, and business-to-business, trial relates to obtaining new customers.

Obtain Repeat Usage after Initial Trial. If your company has obtained high degrees of initial trial, it is important to make sure you establish continuity of purchase and loyalty. Often large amounts of trial exist, but the repeat purchase ratio is very low. If this is the case, establish an objective of increased repeat purchase and product loyalty, along with a fact finding program to determine why repeat purchase rates are low and what can be done to increase them. Even if repeat purchase rates are fairly strong, there is usually some need to make sure they are maintained. Remember, it is far less expensive and more profitable to keep existing customers than it is to prospect for new ones.

HOW TO DEVELOP MARKETING OBJECTIVES

A worksheet for developing your marketing objectives is provided at the end of this chapter.

Step 1: Review Sales Objectives

The marketing objectives must affect the target market in such a way as to achieve your sales objectives. Since the marketing objectives are quantifiable and measurable, the numerical quantifier used in marketing objectives must be large enough to assure success of the sales goals.

Step 2: Review the Target Market

The size of the potential target market and the current customer base must be known or estimated. (This information should be available from the business review.) This information is necessary because each marketing objective is meant to affect the target market's behavior. The marketer must know the number of customers being affected, or it will be impossible to estimate the effect of marketing objectives on sales.

Step 3: Review of Problems and Opportunities

Solving the problems and exploiting the opportunities will be the basis for your marketing objectives. If you find that trial is low but retrial is very high, you might focus your objectives on new customers. If, on the other hand, your company is not obtaining repeat purchase or dollar per purchase levels equal to those of your competitors, you might focus on existing customers when developing marketing objectives.

Step 4: Formulate a Rationale

The rationale allows you to determine whether your marketing objectives will actually allow you to meet your sales objectives. In the example on the following page (Exhibit 6.1), the marketing goals of 10 percent new trial from new users and 60 percent repeat from the new users who tried the product were tested to see if the sales goal increase of $25,000,000 was achievable. In order to analyze this, target market size, total repeat usage, and price of product must be determined. The math and logic of this example is straightforward. You should develop a similar rationale for your marketing objectives to make certain they are providing what is needed to accomplish your sales objectives.

MARKETING STRATEGIES	### Definition A *marketing strategy* is a statement detailing how an individual marketing objective will be achieved. It describes the method for accomplishing the objective. While marketing objectives are specific, quantifiable, and measurable, marketing strategies are *descriptive*. They explain how the measurable objectives will be met.
HOW TO DEVELOP MARKETING STRATEGIES	A worksheet for devloping your marketing strategies is provided at the end of this chapter. Marketing objectives are very narrow in scope, relating to customer behavior. Marketing strategies are broader and provide direction for all areas of the marketing plan. Marketing strategies serve as a guide to the positioning of your product. They also serve as reference points for the development of specific marketing mix tool programs later in the marketing plan (product, price, distribution, personal selling/operations, promotion, advertising message, advertising media, merchandising, and publicity). However, marketing

EXHIBIT 6.1 Developing Your Marketing Objective Rationale

Sales Goal	Increase dollar sales 10 percent over the previous year, from $250MM to $275MM
Target Market	Women age 18+
Total potential target market size	85MM (Does not include existing customers)
Marketing goal	10% New trial; 60% Repeat users from new users
Total new users	85MM x 10% = 8.5MM New users
Repeat users	60% x 8.5MM = 5.1MM Repeat users
Repeat usage by customers	4 Times per year (2 timers per year in this calculation because not all new customers will be users for the full year)
Average price of product	$1.33
Total sales	8.5MM x 1 Time use @ $1.33 = $11.3MM 5.1MM x 2 Repurchases @ $1.33 = $13.6MM Total Sales = $24.9MM

Note: This calculation is to determine if additional sales of approximately $25MM will be achieved.
    It is assumed that the previous sales level will be maintained through existing customers.

strategies do not provide such specifics as "use television," which belongs in the actual media segment of the marketing plan. You should review each of the following categories and determine whether you need to address the topic by developing one or more marketing strategies. (Note: All of the following categories may not apply to your particular firm.)

Build the Market or Steal Market Share?

A critical strategic decision facing all marketers writing a plan will be whether you plan to *build the market* or *steal share* from competitors in order to achieve your sales goals. A situation with a relatively new product where the current user base is small, the potential user base is quite large, and there is little competition often requires a build the market strategy. The company that creates the market often maintains the largest market share into the future. An example of this would be Miller Lite beer. Miller established the light beer category and has been the market share leader ever since. However, remember that it is usually easier to steal market share than to build the market. Building market share takes additional time and money because it is a two-step process. You have to develop consumers' need for the product and then convince them to purchase your product.

Conversely, a situation where the product is a mature one with little growth (i.e., few new customers entering the marketplace) often calls for stealing market share from competitors. In this situation you have to convince product category users that your product is superior to that of your competition.

This is a fundamental strategic decision that must be made up front in your marketing strategy section. The decision whether to build the market or steal share will affect all other areas of the marketing plan. A stealing share strategy such as "steal market share from the leading competitor" requires that your company's target market definitions closely approximate those of the current market leader's customer profile. Also, the advertising will most likely communicate benefits or an image of your product the market leader doesn't possess. To the contrary, a build the market strategy often requires educating new customers about the benefits of product usage and convincing them first to use the product category, and only then to use your company's products.

Strategy Examples

Build the market for Nolan Foods through educating the target market of the superior health and taste properties of the new Nolan product.

Steal share from the premium segment of the green and ripe olive category.

National, Regional, and Local Market Strategies

This strategy helps the marketer determine whether there will be a core national marketing plan or a combination of national, regional, and local marketing plans.

Strategy Examples

Develop an umbrella national marketing support program executed from the home office with individualized local marketing programs executed by each local sales office.

Place incremental local marketing emphasis against the markets that had flat or declining sales last year.

Develop a unified national marketing program with all efforts being leveraged against one common advertising campaign and dealer sell-in program.

In addition to the national marketing program, develop a local dealer marketing program with "turn key" marketing programs (from "how-tos" to creative material for implementation) designed to meet specific objectives (increase trial, increase retrial, increase dollar per transaction, etc.).

Seasonality Strategies

Strategic decisions must be made concerning when to advertise or promote your product, service, or store.

Strategy Examples

Place the greatest marketing efforts and execute mass media marketing programs during the strongest selling months. First maximize the months with the most opportunity before trying to develop the poorer selling months.

Build the month of December, a month that performs relatively poorly for the company but is one of the strongest months for the product category nationally.

Due to the short peak selling season, develop marketing and communication programs that lead the selling season so the effect can be felt early in the season and repeat business can be maximized.

Competitive Strategies

Often there is need for a competitive strategy. The business review may reveal that a single competitor is almost totally responsible for your company's decline in market share; or a single company or group of competitors may have preempted your unique positioning in the marketplace. If this is the case, you will need to develop a competitive marketing strategy in your marketing plan.

Strategy Examples

Preempt the domination Competitor X has on the value attribute by stressing the superior price/quality relationship in all integrated marketing communication activities.

Minimize Competitor Z's entry into the market by heavily promoting the three months prior to Z's grand opening, specifically targeting Competitor Z's trading area.

Target Market Strategies

Your target market section detailed primary and secondary target markets. You must now discuss the emphasis you will place on the various target markets and how you will market to them.

Strategy Examples

Target the heavy user through the emphasis of the high performance product line.

Target only the heavy users—those dealers that account for over 70 percent of the company's business.

Target women with children through emphasis of providing value on athletic shoes—the dominant kid's shoe and an important part of the women's casual shoe purchases.

Initiate in-store changes that appeal to the heavy user: more fashion, higher end goods, and better service to help make for a more time efficient shopping experience.

Target the primary target market through the entire spectrum of marketing mix tools. Target the secondary target market through in-store incentives only.

Consolidate the target market of age 18 to 34 through use of targeted line extensions and more promotional appeals to induce initial trial. In addition, develop a closer relationship with this narrower target by identifying more closely with its unique lifestyle.

Product Strategies

Primarily, the product areas that need strategic consideration include new product, product line extensions, product improvement, and product elimination. Product strategy considerations also include the decision to build or improve weaker product lines from a sales standpoint or continue to maximize stronger selling product lines.

Strategy Examples

Expand alternative use of the product to develop the newly defined target market of adults age 55 plus.

Continue to build and emphasize the stronger performing products—place the vast majority of spending and advertising emphasis behind these products. In addition, use the popularity of the top 10 products—cross sell from stronger selling products to weaker selling products.

Eliminate products that have not become profitable after five years in the marketplace.

Branding Strategies

If you are going to develop a new name for your company or product, a general branding strategy and branding parameters should be included.

Branding Example

Devlop a new propeller name that reflects the superior performance of the five-blade propeller.

Packaging Strategies

If you are going to develop packaging for a new product or update a current package plan, establish a general packaging direction for this segment later in the marketing plan.

Strategy Examples

Change the packaging to make it more noticeable at the point-of-purchase.

Utilize the packaging to help increase repeat purchase among current customers.

Pricing Strategies

You need to address whether you will use a high price, parity, or low price strategy relative to the marketplace or a specific competitor. Also, many times there is a pricing strategy relating to the positioning (i.e., utilizing price to reinforce the positioning).

Strategy Examples

Utilize a parity price strategy in the weaker selling months with a lower price than the market share leader during the strong seasonal selling periods.

Establish a premium price consistent with the premium product positioning.

Distribution of Product/Penetration or Coverage Strategies

The strategic decisions that must be made in this area are different for package goods and business-to-business firms than for those of retailers and service firms. Package goods and business-to-business firms must decide in what areas of the country to target their distribution efforts. They also must decide the type of outlet that will carry their product and the desired market coverage among the targeted outlet category.

Retailers and service firms must decide whether marketing objectives can be achieved through existing outlets, whether new stores can be added in existing markets without cannibalizing existing stores, or whether new stores need to be added through opening new markets.

Strategy Examples

Do not expand to any new markets until existing markets have been fully penetrated.

Concentrate on gaining incremental distribution in the Northeast.

Place additional emphasis on markets where the category has demonstrated strong sales but the company's product has not done as well as expected (strong potential markets).

Personal Selling/Operation Strategies

You need to determine whether your organization will incorporate a structured personal selling program in its marketing plan.

Strategy Examples

Develop specific sales ratios (number of specific prospects that become customers for manufacturers and number of purchasers versus walkers for retailers) to help monitor the effectiveness of the sales force.

Provide a strong and innovative incentive program to reward goal oriented individuals.

Promotion Strategies

Promotions should be channeled to meet specific needs and incorporated into the overall marketing plan in a disciplined fashion. The promotion strategies in this marketing section will set the areas of emphasis for the specific promotion plan later in the marketing plan.

Strategy Examples

Achieve multiple purchases through in-store promotions.

Utilize trade promotion to help establish the selling of the brand to the trade.

Utilize promotion to encourage purchase during the weaker seasonal months.

Spending Strategies

Spending strategies detail how the marketing dollars will be spent. To achieve your marketing objectives, you need to decide whether to increase sales of weaker selling brands, stores, or regions of the country, or to attract more customers to your stronger brands or stores. In order to make these decisions, you need to determine spending levels by brand, store, market, or regions of the country.

Overall spending should also be addressed. Does your company plan to spend at a percent of sales for marketing and advertising consistent with past years? Or because of new aggressive sales projections and marketing objectives, do you need to increase marketing and advertising spending from, for example, 4.2 percent of gross sales to 6 percent? The actual spending detail will be highlighted in the budget section of the marketing plan.

Strategy Examples

Increase advertising spending as a percent of sales to be competitive with the market leader.

Spend at significantly higher levels against the top three selling products, maximizing their growth potential.

Advertising Message Strategies

The marketer needs to provide an overall focus for the advertising and communication. It is important to state up front in your marketing strategy section how you will use advertising to fulfill your marketing objectives.

Strategy Examples

Develop image advertising to build long-term sales and brand loyalty.

Focus on promotional advertising, emphasizing short-term traffic and sales.

Vary the advertising message by region, effectively communicating different benefits depending on the needs of the region.

Develop both a national image campaign and a local market-by-market advertising campaign that is more promotional in focus.

Advertising Media Strategies

The strategies developed in this section should be consistent with the direction established in the product, competitive, and spending marketing strategies. The primary goal in establishing an overall media strategy is to provide direction for the upcoming media plan while also establishing geographic and product spending emphasis.

Strategy Examples

Invest in new markets to establish awareness and generate trial.

Spend heavier in markets with a high potential for growth and with adequate penetration.

Merchandising Strategies

A strategy is needed to set the tone for what will be done from a merchandising standpoint. This applies, for example, to in-store signage and staff uniforms for retailers, point-of-purchase displays and trade brochures for package goods firms, and devices such as brochures, personal sales devices, and sell sheets for business-to-business firms. It also includes special events for all three business categories.

Strategy Examples

Utilize extensive point-of-purchase merchandising to affect decision making in-store.

Utilize merchandising to help draw attention to the package in-store.

Provide the sales force with communication support materials to help close the sale.

Publicity Strategies

You should determine if you are going to make publicity part of your marketing plan. If you are, your publicity effort should be channeled early in the marketing plan. Then there will be an overall direction established when it comes time to develop a specific publicity plan later in the marketing plan.

Strategy Examples

Use media co-sponsors and planned events to generate publicity.

Develop a publicity program to obtain articles in the leading trade publications.

Marketing Research and Development (R&D) Strategies

A disciplined program to meet the continual changes in the marketplace is critical. In most businesses there is a need to continually expand or refine the company's product offering and marketing efforts to build incremental sales. This can be accomplished through a planned and disciplined research and development program.

Marketing R&D is the lifeblood in perpetuating the success of your business. It takes work, planning, and perseverance to test and produce readable results, but it is always worth it. It keeps you ahead of the competition and helps you avoid costly mistakes. Testing can help you develop a new product or marketing activity, make it better, measure your program's effectiveness, and eliminate ineffective ideas before a costly investment has been made.

Once you have committed to some form of marketing R&D, this section should be used to define what you will be testing: new products, services, merchandising programs, store layouts, packaging, media strategies, advertising messages, pricing, promotions, etc. Then fully develop each test program in the respective marketing mix tool objective and strategy sections later in the marketing plan.

Strategy Examples

Institute a marketing testing program to develop new product alternatives.

Develop a marketing R&D program to determine the optimum media mix.

Primary Research Strategies

If you plan to conduct primary research, now is the time to establish a research strategy. You may develop a research strategy to solve a specific problem that will help you build sales and accomplish a marketing objective. Or you may decide to conduct an ongoing awareness, attitude, and behavior tracking study to assist with next year's plan and to provide a benchmark to evaluate the results of current and future marketing plans.

Strategy Examples

Develop an ongoing tracking study to monitor consumer awareness, attitudes, and behavior.

Summary

1: Review Problems and Opportunities

Again, go back and review your problems and opportunities. First, read through the list and make notes of your ideas on how to solve the problems and take advantage of the opportunities. Be as creative as possible in this exercise, coming up with multiple solutions for each problem or opportunity.

2: Review Marketing Objectives

Review your marketing objectives. Now reread the problems and opportunities, along with your original notes on how to solve the problems and take advantage of the opportunities. Determine which of the ideas will form strategies capable of achieving the marketing objectives.

3: Develop Marketing Strategies

Make certain that you have developed strategies to cover each of the strategic categories that are necessary to fulfill your marketing objectives. The strategies should provide the direction for use of the marketing mix tools throughout the marketing plan. You will develop specific plans for these strategies later in your advertising, media, promotion, and marketing mix tool sections. You may have a seasonality strategy to emphasize the stronger selling periods with mass communications and the weaker selling periods with in-store promotions. A spending strategy may be to grow and develop specific markets at the expense of established markets. Both of these strategies will be reflected later in the detailed media plan.

In summary, after reading the marketing strategies, upper management should have a good idea of how you will achieve your marketing objectives from a strategic standpoint. However, the details of these strategies will be fully developed in the subsequent marketing mix tool sections of the marketing plan.

Worksheet 6.1

Marketing Objectives

Short-Term Objectives

Rationale

Long-Term Objectives

Rationale

Worksheet 6.2   Marketing Strategies

Build the Market or Steal Market Share Strategies

Rationale

National, Regional, and Local Marketing Strategies

Rationale

Branding Strategies

Rationale

Seasonality Strategies

Rationale

Worksheet 6.2

Marketing Strategies (Continued)

Competitive Strategies

Rationale

Target Market Strategies

Rationale

Product Strategies

Rationale

Packaging Strategies

Rationale

Worksheet 6.2   Marketing Strategies (Continued)

Pricing Strategies

Rationale

Distribution of Product/Store Penetration Strategies

Rationale

Personal Selling/Operation Strategies

Rationale

Promotion Strategies

Rationale

Worksheet 6.2

Spending Strategies

Rationale

Advertising Message Strategies

Rationale

Advertising Media Strategies

Rationale

Merchandising Strategies

Rationale

Worksheet 6.2   Marketing Strategies (Continued)

Publicity Strategies

Rationale

Marketing R&D Strategies

Rationale

Primary Research Strategies

Rationale

Positioning Strategy

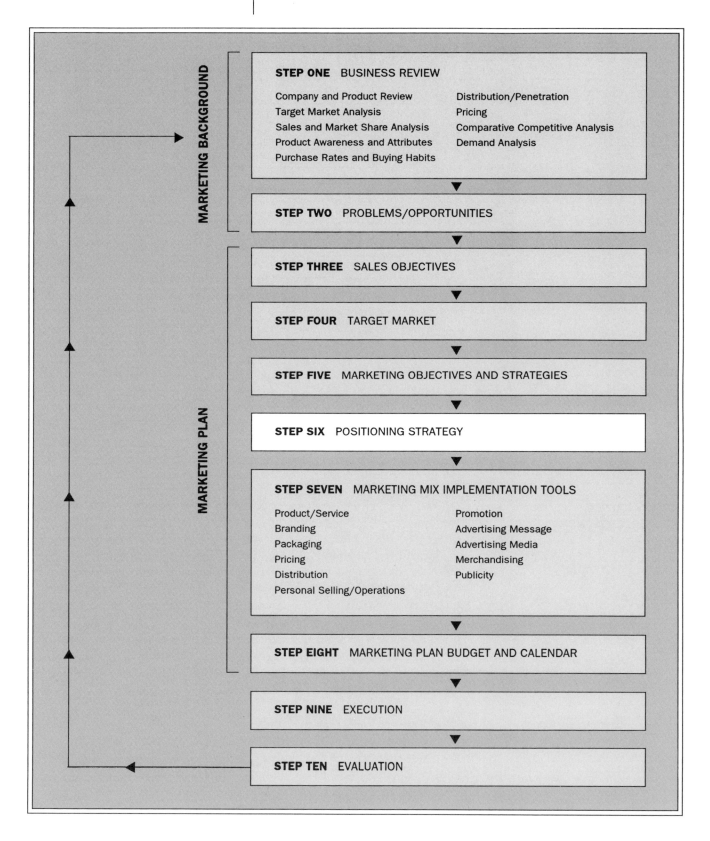

MARKETING BACKGROUND

STEP ONE   BUSINESS REVIEW

Company and Product Review
Target Market Analysis
Sales and Market Share Analysis
Product Awareness and Attributes
Purchase Rates and Buying Habits

Distribution/Penetration
Pricing
Comparative Competitive Analysis
Demand Analysis

STEP TWO   PROBLEMS/OPPORTUNITIES

MARKETING PLAN

STEP THREE   SALES OBJECTIVES

STEP FOUR   TARGET MARKET

STEP FIVE   MARKETING OBJECTIVES AND STRATEGIES

STEP SIX   POSITIONING STRATEGY

STEP SEVEN   MARKETING MIX IMPLEMENTATION TOOLS

Product/Service
Branding
Packaging
Pricing
Distribution
Personal Selling/Operations

Promotion
Advertising Message
Advertising Media
Merchandising
Publicity

STEP EIGHT   MARKETING PLAN BUDGET AND CALENDAR

STEP NINE   EXECUTION

STEP TEN   EVALUATION

Positioning

The next step in your planning process is to develop a market positioning for your product, service, or store. The positioning process is both fun and frustrating, because it calls for creative thinking on one hand and a sorting out of multiple sets of data on the other. Be open-minded and visionary; think as a buyer rather than a seller.

DEFINITION

Once you have defined your target markets and have established marketing objectives and strategies, you must develop a market positioning for your product. By positioning, you create an image in the minds of the target market, establishing the *desired perception of your product relative to the competition.*

IMPORTANCE OF POSITIONING

No matter what you are marketing, a salient positioning is necessary. It is the basis for all your communications: branding, advertising, promotion, packaging, sales force, merchandising, and publicity. By having one meaningful, targeted positioning as a guide for all your communications, you will convey a consistent image. Each vehicle of communication conveying a common positioning will reinforce the others for a cumulative effect, maximizing the return of your marketing investment. Accordingly, everything you do from a marketing perspective must *reinforce one positioning.* Otherwise, you will not only undermine your marketing efforts but confuse the target group as well. Because of the inclusivity of positioning, you must look for a positioning that is not only right for your product now but will also be adaptable years into the future for both the marketplace and the product.

Positioning Considerations

In order to arrive at a successful long-term positioning, you must consider the inherent drama of the product you are selling, the needs and wants of the target markets, and the competition. The business review and the problems and opportunities you have completed, along with the target market determination and marketing strategies you developed, are key to arriving at the right positioning.

You must understand the strengths and weaknesses of your product versus that of the competition. Where is your product comparable to the competition and where is it different? Where is it unique? And most important, what do these competitive differences, if any, mean to the target market? If the positioning reflects a difference that your product cannot deliver or that is not important to the target group, your positioning will not be successful. And even if your product possesses a meaningful difference, your positioning will not be effective if the target group does not perceive it as meaningfully different. As you develop your product positioning, you must deal with the target group's *perception* of the competing products even though it is not altogether accurate, because they are the buyers, and consequently *their perception is truth.*

You must closely evaluate how your product ties to the target market relative to the competition in order to arrive at a specific positioning. To help you position your own product, you can use the matching or mapping step-by-step methods.

POSITION BY MATCHING

Simply stated, this positioning method matches your product's inherent and unique benefits or competitive advantage to the characteristics and needs/wants of the target market.

Step 1: Analyze Your Product versus the Competition

A good place to start with this method is with the product you are selling and the competition you are selling against. Based on your business review, list your competition on the top left side of the worksheet provided at the end of this chapter (also see Exhibit 7.1 shown after Step 5). The competition could be one major competitor, a number of key competitors, a specific category, or a number of key categories. In the positioning of an off-price menswear retailer, it was determined that specific competition varied by market, but the competitive categories remained the same in all markets: department stores, specialty men's clothing stores, and off-price/discount stores.

Step 2: Identify Product Differences versus Competition

Next, write down the key positive and negative differences of your product versus that of the competition relative to your primary target market. These differences should be listed as they relate to key elements of the marketing mix that are appropriate to what you are selling. Sometimes a difference, although seemingly negative, can become a positive. A small retailer with limited square footage and thereby limited in variety of product offering can lead to a positioning of specialty selection and personal attention.

For Coors, a meaningful difference was quality; their beer is unpasteurized and fresh, with the beer shipped from the brewery refrigerated. For Cheer, it is the one laundry detergent that washes all types of clothes in hot, warm, or cold water ("All Tempercheer"). For Funny Face powdered soft drink, the children oriented name was the key, which led back to a pure kids positioning. For a retail ski client, being new to a market and offering many innovative customer services led to its positioning as the "new age of ski shops." This was a very appropriate positioning, because the skiing target market was young adult, contemporary, and into "change." For a business-to-business firm selling to office supply stores, its established reputation and many office product innovations led to a leadership positioning, "Organizing the American office since 1949."

For each area, ask yourself, "How is my product different and how is it better?" Is your product different through product superiority, innovation, or size—number of customers, volume of goods sold, number of outlets? Whenever possible, use quantitative research for objectivity.

Step 3: List Your Key Target Market

Insert your key target market on the top right side of the same worksheet (see Exhibit 7.1).

Step 4: List Key Target Market Characteristics

On the right side of the worksheet, now list the characteristics of your target market in terms of wants and needs. With or without research, ask yourself the following questions, listing brief answers below each question:

- *What is the target market really purchasing?* Is the product to be used by itself or in conjunction with a number of products (e.g., are women purchasing dress shoes separately or as part of a fashion ensemble)? For what purpose is the target using the product (e.g., is the baking soda for baking a cake, deodorizing the refrigerator, or brushing teeth)?

- *Where is the target market purchasing/using it?* By geography (e.g., in sunny, very warm climates) and by place (e.g., in the home, car, etc.)?

- *When is the target market using it?* Time of the year, month, week, day, during or after work?

- *Why is the target market purchasing and/or using the product or why are they purchasing from one store over the other?* Is it because of a particular feature? Is it convenient location or greater selection? Why are they really using the product? Does it save time or money?

- *How is it purchased/used?* Is it purchased/used alone or with other people? Is it a frequent or infrequent purchase? How is it used (e.g., is the tissue used to wipe one's nose or clean the windows? Is the beer used to relax after work or celebrate and party)?

- *How is the target changing?* Is the market changing by demographics and lifestyle? How are purchasing/usage habits of the product changing (e.g., is fashion becoming more important than durability, value more than price, service more than just product quality)?

Step 5: Match Your Product's Characteristics to the Target Market's Needs/Wants

Having listed the differences of your product below the key competition and listed the key needs/wants of the target market, try to match what is unique about your product to the meaningful needs and wants of the target market. Using a retail fabric chain as an example, in Exhibit 7.1 we have listed the specific competition and retailer's competitive differences on the left and the target market and its characteristics on the right.

Based on the listing of the competitive differences, it would appear that this fabric retailer has a competitive advantage through offering an abundance of fabric related merchandise in larger, better designed stores. The merchandise selection appears superior not only in amount but in the variety of merchandise necessary to complete a sewing project, as well as related crafting and home decorating projects. Also, this retailer could be viewed as a leader with an established reputation offering a variety of quality merchandise but *not* at the lowest prices or greatest values.

The target market, on the other hand, is a mix of both practically and recreationally motivated sewers who want a large selection of all types of fabric related merchandise that is very competitively priced and is a real value. It would seem that this retailer definitely has the desired selection and quality but not necessarily the lower prices and value. The target also wants all the required merchandise under one roof to enjoy a fun and rewarding shopping experience, as well as fulfill the needs for both practically and recreationally motivated projects.

Further, the listing indicates changes occurring within the target market. It appears sewers have less time or need to sew regularly, creating fewer garments and becoming more recreationally oriented with a growing interest in craft and home decorating projects.

After reviewing both sides of your worksheet again and again, you hope to find a competitive advantage or advantages coming together to match a clustering of the target's current and changing needs. In this retail fabric chain example, there appear to be a number of competitive advantages coming together under a "superior selection offering" (wide variety, quality, fashionable, growing selection, and larger stores). These advantages would appear to match the target's growing desire for a fabric store with a large and complete offering of not just sewing but craft and home decorating merchandise.

By matching the key differences to the key target market needs/wants of the positioning listings, you could arrive at the following positioning statement for this fabric retail chain: "Each store provides *everything* a woman needs to fulfill fabric related sewing, crafting, and home decorating expectations."

After you have prepared your positioning worksheet, if it helps, draw lines from the major competitive positive differences to the paralleling want/need characteristics of the target market. Then ask yourself again what really is important to the target market in terms of how your product is different and better. Based on this, eliminate lines until you have the two or three most meaningful product to target market potential positioning connections.

In some cases you might combine two product differences or advantages to fill an important want. If you were a retailer, you may combine the attributes of brand name products and very competitive prices to arrive at a *value* positioning that ties to an important consumer desire.

In some cases you will draw lines between product and target market characteristics and find that a most important consumer need/want is not being fulfilled by your product or the competition. Virginia Slims was created to fill a consumer void or gap with a cigarette for women. Or, to the other extreme, all the competing products available fulfilled the target's need/want, but no one competitor, including your product, has claimed it as their reason for being.

EXHIBIT 7.1 Positioning: Matching Product Differences to the Target Market's Needs/Wants

Competition
1. Specialty chains
2. Mass merchants

Differences from Competitor
Product/Store/Service Attributes
    Larger selection of fabrics and notions
    Slightly better quality
    Favorite store of sewers
    Always new merchandise
    Carries variety of goods for sewing, home decorating, and crafting

New Products/Improvements
    Greater expansion into craft and home decorating merchandise

Packaging/Store Appearance
    Best store layout
    Larger stores
    Does not have promotional appearance

Branding/Name/Reputation
    Established reputation

Distribution/Penetration
    Greater number of outlets in most markets

Price
    Perception of higher prices and less value

Advertising
    Have more advertising

Key Target Market
Practical and recreation sewers
Women age 25-54
Average household income
3+ household size

Characteristics—Needs/Wants
What
    Wide selection of merchandise from which to choose
    Be able to purchase everything at one store
    Lowest prices/good values
    Quality fabrics

Where
    Sew at home

When
    After work and weekends (seen as recreation)
    Throughout the day (considered part of family responsibilities by practical sewers)

Why (Benefit)
    For fun and as a hobby
    To express creativity
    For herself and children
    To save money
    For better fit of garments
    For feeling of accomplishment

How Purchased/Used
    Usually shop alone
    Visit a fabric store on average every two weeks
    Like to shop for deals
    Shop for enjoyment

How the Target and Its Needs/Wants Are Changing
    Less sewing to save money
    More sewing for fun and recreation
    Not enough time to sew
    More sewers working out of the home
    Using fabrics not just for sewing garments but for more crafting and decorating the home
    Buying more fabric related merchandise for special occasions/holidays

POSITION BY MAPPING

This approach is a practical application of mapping methodology based on multidimensional models. Although theoretical in origin, we actively use the mapping approach in the positioning of our clients' products and services. Using this approach, you map out visually what is important to your target market in terms of key product attributes. The competition's products, including your own, are then ranked on these attributes. This type of mapping is extremely useful in positioning a product and, again, is *most effective when based on quantitative research that is representative of the marketplace.* Your preconceived notions about what the target market thinks can differ dramatically from what quantifiable research reports.

However, if you do not have market research, it is still helpful to use this method when positioning to help sort out what you believe is important to the target market. Further, this positioning approach will help you to more clearly evaluate how well your product and that of your key competition is perceived on each attribute. Because this mapping method is somewhat involved and you will most likely not have research to assist you, read through the three steps before beginning the actual mapping process.

Step 1: List Product Attributes by Importance

Acknowledging your built-in bias while being as objective as possible, the first step is to list in order of importance the product category attributes on the right side of the mapping worksheet provided at the end of this chapter (see also Exhibit 7.2 shown after Step 3) top to bottom, from most important (10 value) to least important (1 value).

In the retail category, the most important attribute to the consumer might be quality, followed by selection, price, service, and fashion, with location listed at the bottom. In business-to-business it might be reliable delivery ranked most important, followed by product consistency, quality, price, and favorable reputation, with knowledgeable sales force being least important at the bottom of the chart.

Step 2: Rate Your Product and Competitors' Products for Each Attribute

Once you have listed the key target market attributes, for each attribute rate each competitor from best to worst. For each rating, place the initial of each key competitor, including your product, on the line of each attribute ranking. Make a master listing of these keys under company/product/store code.

If you do not have available quantitative research before you begin mapping, it's a good idea to gather a number of people knowledgeable about your product category and have each one list the most important attributes. Next, have them, as objectively as possible, independently assign a number from 1 to 10 (10 being most important, 1 least important) for each attribute. Take an average of these estimates for each ranking. Based on each composite estimate, rank order the attributes.

After ranking attribute importance, ask the participants to agree on the top three to five market competitors, including your product. Then have each of them independently assign a rating of 1 to 10 for each competitor on each attribute, with 10 being best. Average the ratings for each competitor, and insert a rating for each competitor by initial in line with each attribute ranking.

In your plotting of the competitive market, you might have great disparity between competitors on one attribute and no differences on another. Ideally, you want your product ranked the best versus the competition on all attributes, but particularly on those that are most important to the consumer. The more you see your product's initial on the right, particularly on those attributes at the top of the chart, the stronger the position of your product in the marketplace.

A note of caution: Using a knowledgeable group of people to assist in arriving at key attributes and competitive ratings is not very accurate compared to using survey research that will quantify the perceptions of the users and/or purchasers. However, with no research available, this approach will at least give you more perspective than if you just positioned by matching.

Step 3: Visualize Desired Position on Map for Your Product

Once your positioning map is complete, review how your product ranks on the more important attributes relative to the competition. Next, visualize where you want your product positioned on the map based on what the consumer wants and what your product can provide relative to strengths and weaknesses of the competition. Finally, from the various types of positionings previously discussed, select the positioning approach that will positively affect the target market's perceptions and attain your visualized positioning.

To illustrate, we will use one of our clients as a case example. In Exhibit 7.2, our client, a very price oriented retailer with the code letter H, rated second to last competitively on the two most important attributes for the retail category: quality and value. Declining sales had prompted the store chain to do market research among consumers. This research indicated, among other things, that although price was important, quality and value were most important. Based on this data, the company changed its position from a "store with low prices" to "the value shoe store"—a store with quality merchandise at competitive prices. Translating this goal to the map visually would mean it would be the first store from the right for the value attribute. Accordingly, this retailer upgraded its merchandise mix and the appearance of its stores. The advertising was also changed to convey a value image.

The results of this value positioning versus the former low price/discount price positioning were dramatic. Comparable store sales for the year increased more than 30 percent. Market research conducted 18 months after the benchmark research study revealed dramatic positive shifts in how the consumer perceived this retailer versus the competition on the key attributes. As you can see in Exhibit 7.3, the retailer's competitive rating (H) on *quality* moved from second to last to second. Further, its competitive *value* rating moved from second to last to first, while the *price* rating remained virtually the same. Even the retailer's competitive rating on *selection* showed considerable positive movement from third to second place.

EXHIBIT 7.2 Original Price Positioning

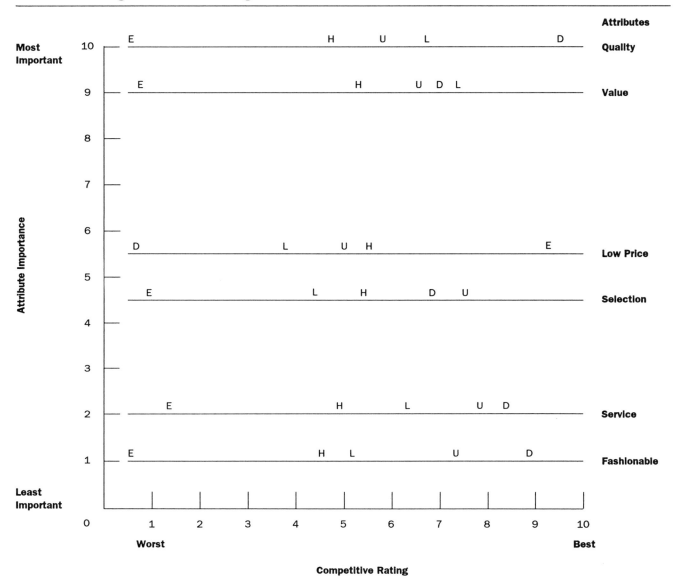

HOW TO WRITE THE POSITIONING STRATEGY

Once you have determined how you want your product perceived by the target market as meaningfully different from the competition, you are ready to write alternative positioning strategies. It is wise to write more than one positioning strategy in order to compare strategy statements and evaluate which positioning best reflects your product relative to the competition and fulfills the needs/wants of the target market. Your alternative positioning statements should vary by the degree of emphasis placed on the product advantage, the competition's weakness, and the target market benefit. All of the positioning alternatives relate to product, competitor, and target market, but each alternative will focus on one of the above rather than all.

EXHIBIT 7.3 Original Price versus New Value Positioning*

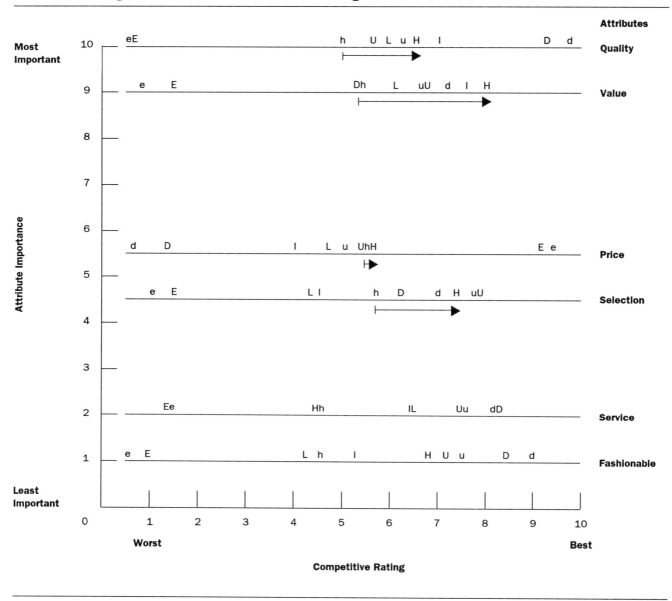

*Lowercase letters represent original positioning; uppercase letters represent new positioning.

The key word is *focus* when writing a positioning statement. The tendency is to write a positioning statement that reads like a litany rather than keeping it simple and straightforward. The shorter and more to the point, the better the positioning strategy. A succinct positioning will provide clear and specific direction for the advertising and the employment of all the other tools in the marketing mix. For this reason, choose thoughtfully each word that you use in your positioning statement.

Once you have prepared the alternative positionings, select the one that will best suit the target market and fulfill the marketing strategies using the format provided at the end of this chapter. Below, we show some examples of positioning statements.

Retail Shoe Chain

Position Brady's Footwear as the *value alternative* to purchasing shoes at department stores.

- Same quality

- Better selection

- Lower prices

Note that in this positioning strategy, brief qualifiers or descriptors have been included below the positioning statement. This is not always necessary, as you will see from the other examples.

Consumer Package Goods

Position Funny Face as the *kids'* powdered soft drink for summertime fun.

Position Miller Lite as the only beer with superior taste and low caloric content.

Business-to-Business

Position W.T. Jones as the *established office supply leader,* improving the look and efficiency of the office environment.

Worksheet 7.1

Positioning: Matching Product Differences to the Target Market's Needs/Wants

Key Competition

1

2

3

Differences from Competitor

Product/Store/Service Attributes/Benefits

New Products/Improvements

Packaging/Store Appearance

Branding/Name/Reputation

Distribution/Penetration

Price

Advertising (Message/Media)

Promotion

Merchandising

Personal Selling and Service

Publicity

Key Target Market

Characteristics—Needs/Wants

What

Where

When

Why (Benefit)

How Purchased/Used

How the Target and Its Needs/Wants Are Changing

Worksheet 7.2

Positioning: Mapping Product Importance by Competitive Ranking

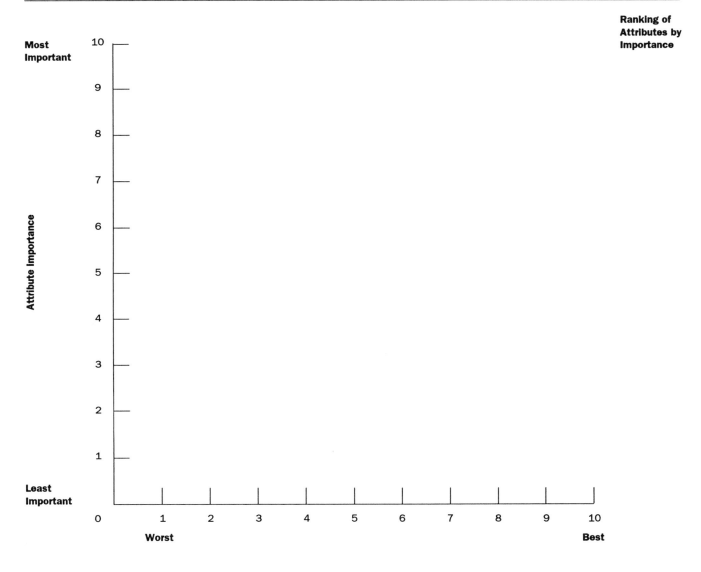

Ranking of Attributes by Importance

Most Important — 10

Least Important

Attribute Importance

Competitive Rating

0 1 2 3 4 5 6 7 8 9 10

Worst — Best

Company/Product/Store/Service and Code Letters

Name   Code

Worksheet 7.3

Positioning Strategy

Strategy Statement

Qualifier/Descriptors (Only If Necessary)

Rationale

STEP SEVEN | Marketing Mix Implementation Tools

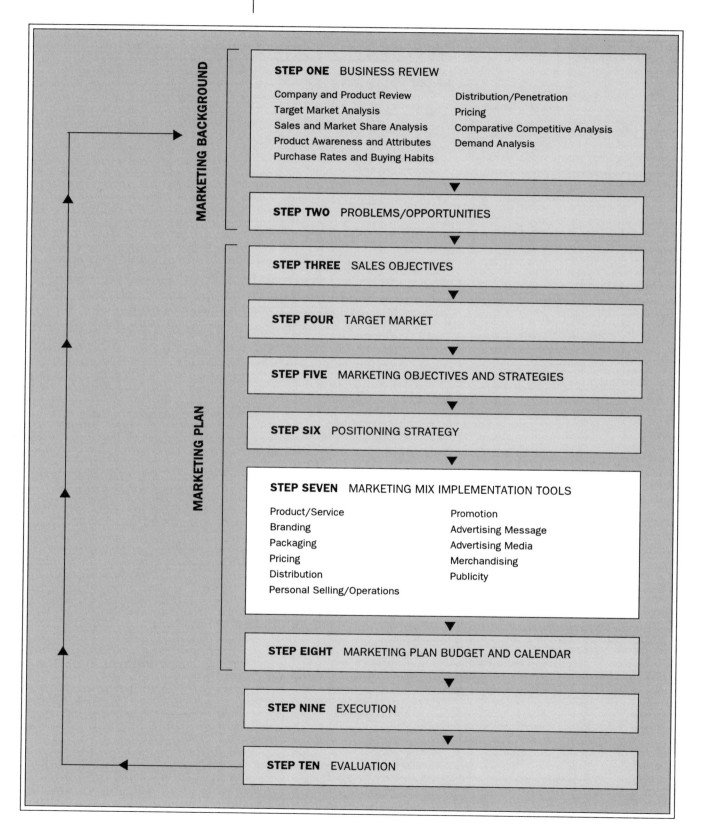

MARKETING BACKGROUND

STEP ONE BUSINESS REVIEW

Company and Product Review
Target Market Analysis
Sales and Market Share Analysis
Product Awareness and Attributes
Purchase Rates and Buying Habits

Distribution/Penetration
Pricing
Comparative Competitive Analysis
Demand Analysis

STEP TWO PROBLEMS/OPPORTUNITIES

MARKETING PLAN

STEP THREE SALES OBJECTIVES

STEP FOUR TARGET MARKET

STEP FIVE MARKETING OBJECTIVES AND STRATEGIES

STEP SIX POSITIONING STRATEGY

STEP SEVEN MARKETING MIX IMPLEMENTATION TOOLS

Product/Service
Branding
Packaging
Pricing
Distribution
Personal Selling/Operations

Promotion
Advertising Message
Advertising Media
Merchandising
Publicity

STEP EIGHT MARKETING PLAN BUDGET AND CALENDAR

STEP NINE EXECUTION

STEP TEN EVALUATION

Product, Branding, and Packaging

You have just finished developing the positioning for your product. Now you must make sure the product lives up to your planned positioning. Effective communication of a positioning may induce trial of a product, but beware—nothing will ruin a company faster than selling a poor product or a product that is not consistent with its positioning. Customers may be convinced to purchase once, but they won't be fooled again.

The product, the product's brand name, and the product's packaging are the fundamental elements of the entire marketing mix. They make up the reality of the positioning. Since the product is so closely identified with its name and packaging, we have included all three (product, brand or name, and packaging) in one chapter.

PRODUCT

In the case of consumer package goods, retail, and business-to-business companies, the product is a *tangible object* that is marketed to customers. However, for service businesses, the product takes the form of some *intangible offering*. Often for a service business, the product is a future benefit or future promise. Thus, while all products are offerings to the customer, there is an inherent difference between what is sold by a service firm and what is sold by a retailer or manufacturer.

HOW TO DEVELOP A PRODUCT PLAN

A worksheet for developing your product plan is provided at the end of this chapter.

Step 1: Establish Product Objectives

Product objectives will center around one or more of the five following areas:

- Developing new products
- Developing line extensions for existing brands
- Developing new uses for existing products

- Product improvement
- Finding more efficient ways to produce the product in the case of manufacturers or purchase the product in the case of retailers

In addition to addressing one or more of the above, the product objectives should incorporate specifics on when the product will be available for distribution or inventory.

An example of a product objective for a manufacturer would be: "In the upcoming fiscal year, modify the product to reflect the current purchasing habits of consumers interested in low salt foods."

Step 2: Establish Product Strategies

Product strategies define how the product objectives will be accomplished. As an example, the following types of strategies would be developed to meet specific product objectives:

Objective	Strategy Description
Improve the product.	(The marketer would list specific product attributes that would be improved and specific innovations that would bring about improvement.)
Find more efficient ways to produce the product.	(The marketer would list how that would be accomplished, either through a manufacturing technique or a buying practice.)

A specific example of a line extension objective and subsequent strategy for a manufacturer of cross-country skis would be the following:

Objective

Improve the product to take advantage of the consumer trend toward citizen cross-country ski racing.

Strategy

Develop competitively superior performance skis for both cross-country racing methods: track racing and the newly developed skating method.

BRANDING

Branding is the naming of your product, service, or company, with which consumers associate your product. For this reason, a brand or name should help communicate the product's positioning and its inherent drama for the consumer.

HOW TO DEVELOP A BRAND NAME

A worksheet on how to develop your brand name is provided at the end of this chapter.

Step 1: Establish Your Branding Objectives

Branding objectives should state for what the new name will be used (e.g., existing product, new product, product line extension, improved product, repositioned product). Also, the objective should include a final decision date for when the final name will be selected.

Examples of branding objectives are: "Develop a name for the new pizza delivery service by August 1 of this fiscal year." "Develop a new name to replace Big Jake's for the new family apparel store by the end of this fiscal year."

Step 2: Establish Your Branding Strategies

It is important to prepare a branding strategy before developing name alternatives. This greatly increases the probability that you will arrive at a name that is consistent with the product and takes into consideration all of the uses of the name over the short and long term. This strategy should flow from the positioning statement and be followed by a listing of parameters for the new name. The branding strategy should highlight those components that will communicate the key perceptions to the key targets. A branding strategy for the repositioning of Big Jake's from a work clothing store for men to a casual apparel store for families would be: "Rename Big Jake's to describe its *active and casual wear* merchandise, appealing to the woman heavy *purchaser* who is a smart family shopper with an appreciation for quality and saving money."

Step 3: Establish Branding Property Parameters

Along with the branding strategy, include branding property parameters. These are an extension of the branding strategy and provide specific guideposts in name development. Potential branding parameters are:

- Reflects positioning of the product

- Provides generic identification and clearly identifies with its functional category

- Is preemptive

- Contributes to awareness and knowledge of its purpose

- Is memorable

- Provides potential for growth of other entities/line extensions under its umbrella name

- Possesses a positive connotation—meaning, pronunciation, and visualization

- Reflects the personality of the product

- Has intrinsic meaning of its own (i.e., is not an acronym or set of letters that doesn't signify anything)

- Not limited geographically or topically as the organization grows

- Lends itself to/allows for creative development—both visually and in copy

- Must work with current signage/package sizes (the shorter the better)

- Is legally acceptable and protectable

In addition to the actual name, parameters should be set for the name's graphic translation. For example, the name must:

- Graphically reproduce in small and large logo form

- Graphically reproduce in black and white and in color

- Incorporate colors that reflect the positioning and are attention getting

- Have visual impact in both the print and television media

Step 4: Name Generation and Selection

Using the branding strategy and name property parameters as a guide, begin the name development process by generating a multitude of name alternatives. It is conceivable that the name alternatives could number into the hundreds. Next, using the branding strategy and name parameters as the decision criteria in the screening process, pare back the names in a disciplined manner to approximately ten names. Then follow with a legal search of these names for trademark availability. Finally, you would be wise to research the remaining name alternatives with the target markets before making a final branding decision.

PACKAGING

For manufacturers, packaging protects the product and assists in communicating the product's attributes and image. For retailers and service firms, packaging is the inside and outside environment that houses and dispenses the product/services and helps to communicate the company's attributes and image.

HOW TO DEVELOP A PACKAGING PLAN

A worksheet for developing your packaging plan is provided at the end of this chapter.

Step 1: Establish Your Packaging Objectives

Focus packaging objectives on the following:

Manufacturer

Create awareness for your product at the point-of-purchase.

Retailer

Create awareness of the retail facility from the outside through the external store environment and awareness of the products inside through the internal store environment.

Manufacturer and Retailer

- Communicate product attributes and positioning.

- Generate trial.

- Provide protection for the product.

- Allow easy usage of the product.

- Communicate promotional offerings.

- Establish the time frame for development or when the package design will be ready for production.

Examples of product objectives for the manufacturer are as follows:

- Utilize the product's packaging to communicate its family-oriented positioning and the extra servings in each container. Final package design and specifications will be available by the end of this fiscal year.

- Utilize new packaging by the end of this fiscal year to protect the product on the shelf while still allowing consumers to see the rich, vibrant colors of the product.

Step 2: Develop Your Packaging Strategies

Packaging strategies delineate how the objectives will be accomplished, providing specifics such as shape, size, color, copy, design, and, for retailers, overall store environment.

Examples of packaging strategies include:

- Develop a unique and colorful package with simplicity in copy and design that will fit into a floor display and stand out from competitive packaging.

- Communicate leadership through bold colors and larger than life visuals of the product. Highlight product attributes in benefit oriented sentences.

Worksheet 8.1   Product

Product Objectives

Product Strategies

Rationale

Worksheet 8.2

Branding/New Name

Branding Objectives

Branding Strategy

Branding Parameters

Brand/Name Alternatives

Rationale

Worksheet 8.3   Packaging

Packaging Objectives

Packaging Strategies

Rationale

9

Price

The pricing marketing mix tool is one of the most difficult for which to develop a plan. The pricing of your product is critical yet difficult to determine because it must be high enough to cover costs and make a profit for your company, yet low enough to maximize demand and sales potential. In addition, the price of a product affects the product's positioning. For example, a high priced product relative to the competition signals quality and is consistent with products that have special benefits. As you will see in this chapter, pricing plans require flexibility, discipline, and judgment to provide for a pricing structure that is competitive, complements the product's positioning, and maximizes sales *and* profits.

DEFINITION

We will define price for purposes of this book as the monetary value of a product.

HOW TO DEVELOP A PRICING PLAN

A worksheet for developing your pricing plan is provided at the end of this chapter.

Step 1: Establish Your Price Objectives

Price objectives usually focus on the following issues:

- Lower, higher, or parity pricing
- Geography of the pricing
- Timing of the pricing

Lower, Higher, or Parity Pricing

Reviewing your marketing strategies and your pricing problems and opportunities in the context of the following factors will help you determine whether your company should set a higher, lower, or parity price objective.

Lower Price Objective. The reasons for a low price strategy include the following:

- To expand the market, allowing new consumers who couldn't purchase at higher prices to become purchasers.

- To increase trial and/or sales due to price incentives.

- To exploit a situation with a strong price elastic product where a low price results in increased demand. The result is lower margins but increased profits because of the increased volume.

- To preempt competitive strategies, helping to steal market share. This is often necessary in a mature market.

- To remain competitive. If most of the competitors have reduced their prices, you will often need to do so, especially if you are in a price sensitive product category. If a strong competitor is also offering an attribute, such as service, with which you cannot compete, you may need to lower your price to counter the service offering.

- To keep competitors from entering the marketplace by setting a price that is difficult for a new company with high initial investment costs to match. This policy of expanded market pricing allows a company to develop a large, loyal consumer base while keeping competition to a minimum.

Higher Price Objective. Several conditions favor a high price objective, where the price of the product will equate to revenues substantially above the break even point, or the product's price is set above that of the competition.

- To allow fast recovery of the firm's investment.

- To provide faster accumulation of profits to cover R & D costs. The profits can then be used to improve the product and to sustain competitive marketing tactics once competitors enter the market.

- To substantiate a quality image positioning.

- To exploit a situation in which the product is price inelastic, and the demand or sales decrease only marginally with higher pricing.

- To cream profits while there are no substitute products to force competitive pricing. This is typically done for a product or service in the introductory phase of its product life cycle, while representing a substantial innovation within the product category.

- To keep margins high when the company is stressing profits rather than sales.

- To help recover the firm's R & D costs in a short time period, for a product with a short life span. An example would be fad products that last for a relatively short time.

- To exploit a situation in which the product is difficult to copy or has patent protection.

Parity Pricing. Parity pricing is pricing that is comparable to the competition's. It can be effectively used if your product has superior attributes and is priced the same as products with inferior product attributes. It can also effectively be used when your product is similar to your competitors' but there are nonproduct advantages that your company can utilize to provide a better overall value to the consumer. Nonproduct advantages, such as service, guarantees, location for retailers, or distribution channel for manufacturers, are often reasons to purchase, given a parity pricing structure in the marketplace among similar products.

Geography

Many times a company's pricing structure is not uniform across the country. One market may have much greater competition, necessitating lower prices. Or a lower pricing objective may be required in specific markets to help achieve the marketing strategy of developing trial and placing emphasis on certain markets with greater potential. As a result, your pricing objectives should include a description of how you plan to price by geographic regions.

Timing

Finally, timing should be addressed in your price objectives. Do you plan to use a high price, low price, or parity price objective all year, or only during certain portions of the year? Remember that pricing is a tool to help implement marketing strategies and also deliver profits. While timing relates to the changing of your price on a seasonal basis, it also relates to the changing of prices in a timely fashion relative to competitive price changes and to addressing increases or decreases in the margin or cost of goods sold.

Writing the Pricing Objective

The following examples of pricing objectives consider higher or lower price relative to the competition, geography, and timing. "Utilize a lower price relative to the competition throughout the country for the entire year." "Increase prices during the strong tourist months of May to September, then lower prices during the off-season."

Step 2: Establish Your Price Strategies

Pricing strategies state how you will achieve your pricing objectives. They provide the specifics you need to finalize your pricing plan. In developing your pricing strategies, the following steps should be taken.

- *Review your marketing strategies.* It is important to focus on the function of price relative to your other marketing mix tools. Remember, pricing is a tool to help implement and achieve marketing strategies.

- *Review your problems and opportunities.* Especially review Steps 8 and 9 on pricing and competitive analysis of your business review and the subsequent problems and opportunities.

- *Review your pricing mathematics.* Determine at what price you break even. Make certain that if you set a lower price than that of your competition, it will not cause the company to lose money but instead increase sales and profit.

Finally, develop strategies that address how price levels, geography, and timing objectives will be accomplished. Using the information acquired in the three steps above, detail your pricing strategy. Consider the following two marketing strategies.

- *Marketing Seasonality Strategy:* Increase sales among current customers during the off-season.

- *Marketing Pricing Strategy:* Maintain a 45 percent margin for the year.

The *pricing objective* might be to utilize a parity pricing structure relative to the competition during the strong selling season nationally and a low price relative to the competition during the off-season nationally. Price then would be one of the tools used to execute the seasonality marketing strategy along with promotion and advertising. And pricing certainly would be used to execute the pricing marketing strategy.

The subsequent pricing strategies might be as follows:

- Utilize a price consistent with the top three market leaders in the northern markets and the top market leader in the southern markets during the months of August through December.

- Utilize a price at 5 percent below the top three market leaders in the northern markets and 7 percent below the market leader in the southern markets during the off-season of January through July.

Worksheet 9.1   Price

Price Objectives

Rationale

Price Strategies

Rationale

Distribution

Now you need to consider the marketing mix tool of distribution. Up to this point, your efforts have been focused on developing plans to persuade the consumer to purchase your product. Distribution focuses on making sure there is accessible product for the target market to purchase once you have initiated demand.

DEFINITION

We define distribution as the transmission of goods and services from the producer or seller to the user.

HOW TO DEVELOP A DISTRIBUTION PLAN

A worksheet for developing your distribution plan is provided at the end of this chapter.

Step 1: Establish Distribution Objectives

Establish quantifiable distribution objectives for the following four categories:

- Penetration (retailers and service firms) or market coverage/shelf space (manufacturers)

- Type of outlet

- Geography

- Timing

An example for a retail firm would be as follows:

Fully penetrate the firm's two largest markets (Chicago and Detroit, which account for 25 percent of the firm's business) at the rate of one store for every 100,000 households within the next two years (8 stores in this plan year and 10 stores the following year).

Continue to utilize strip centers or freestanding units.

An example for a package goods firm would be as follows:

Improve shelf space to equal that of of the leading competitor in the category.

Step 2: Establish Distribution Strategies

Your distribution strategies should describe how you will accomplish your distribution objectives. The following should be considered by each business category.

Retail and Service Firms

* Describe the criteria or methodology for penetrating markets or adding new locations. Where will you locate new stores? What demographic, location, cost per square foot, competition, or other criteria will you use to make these decisions?

* If you are expanding geographic penetration, specify whether this will be done on a systematic market-by-market basis or wherever the opportunity develops within the total system.

* If a change is warranted, describe how you will make the change from one type of outlet to another.

* Describe your purchase or lease strategies.

Manufacturers

* Describe how you will attain market coverage goals and/or shelf space goals. Some of your strategies to achieve these will be incorporated into your promotional plan. If your business review reveals that your product does not differ from your competition's, your product is not established with the trade, and your product does not make a large impact on the trade in terms of profits, then you will have to rely more heavily on promotions and trade deals to meet aggressive market coverage and shelf space goals.

* If your objective is to increase market coverage, describe how you will choose the type(s) of channel to target for increased coverage and detail specifically what stores you plan to target.

* Outline whether you will use a *push* or *pull* strategy. A push strategy focuses on marketing to the intermediate targets such as distributors and outlets to obtain distribution and shelf space. A pull strategy involves marketing directly to consumers to build demand, forcing the outlets to stock the product.

* Describe how you will enter new distribution channels, if this is an objective. Will you try to place your entire line or one top-selling product in the stores? What kind of merchandising and advertising support will you provide? Will you offer return privileges or lower your minimum order requirements? If storage, display, dispensing, price marking, or accounting specifics are important to the new channel, describe how you will make

allowances to gain distribution trial. Will you provide special introductory pricing?

Assume a distribution objective for a package goods firm is to increase market coverage 20 percent among grocery stores in all top 100 markets over the next year. The strategies to achieve this objective might be:

Place additional sales emphasis against large independents with multiple store outlets.

Concentrate on first establishing the top selling line of frozen foods before attempting to gain distribution of the entire line of frozen and canned foods.

Utilize special promotions developed in the promotion plan to help sell-in product via volume trade deals to encourage initial trial and special introductory pricing incentives.

Worksheet 10.1   Distribution

Distribution Objectives

Distribution Strategies

Rationale

Personal Selling and Operations

Personal selling and operations involve the personal one-on-one contact your company has with the specific target consumer and the day-to-day administration of the selling program, the retail outlet, or the office. Whether it's business-to-business or consumer marketing, personal selling is a very important tool that incorporates the critical human factor into the marketing mix. *It is the one personal and direct link between the target market and your company.*

DEFINITION

In this book, personal selling and operations for retail and service firms involves all functions related to selling in the store, office, or other environments such as door-to-door solicitation, in-home selling, and telemarketing. This includes hiring and managing sales personnel, stocking inventory, preparing the product for sale, as well as the presentation and maintenance of the facility. For business-to-business and package goods firms, personal selling relates to the manufacturers' selling and servicing of its products to the trade or intermediate markets (various buyers of the product within the distribution channel from the original producer to the ultimate user).

HOW TO DEVELOP A PERSONAL SELLING/ OPERATIONS PLAN

A worksheet for developing your personal selling/operations plan is provided at the end of this chapter.

Step 1: Establish Selling/Operations Objectives

Your sales/operations objectives should be as specific as possible; designate a time period for which they apply, and include the following items.

For Retail/Service

- Customer contact—the percentage of store visitors having contact and number of contacts with store staff during a visit

- Customer behavior goals, such as percentage of customers who are persuaded to try on or experience a demonstration of merchandise

- The specific sales ratio

An example of personal selling/operations objectives for a retailer would be:

Establish a minimum of one contact with 90 percent of store visitors and a minimum of two contacts with 50 percent of visitors.

Achieve a 40 percent trial ratio of customers who actually try the merchandise during a hands-on demonstration in-store.

Achieve a 60 percent sales ratio (60 percent of the people who visit the store make a purchase) over the next year during the holiday selling season and a 40 percent sales ratio the rest of the year.

For Manufacturers

- The number and type of companies that must be contacted by the sales force

- The number of sales calls that must be made to each prospect and/or current customer by company type

- The sales ratio (number of contacts versus the number of sales)

- The average sales dollar volume and the number of orders per salesperson per year

- The number of actual product presentations/demonstrations, percentage of product sampling, or trial that must be achieved during sales presentations

- Additional customer behavior goals, such as the percentage of customers who are persuaded to sign up for future sales/product information

Personal selling objective examples for a manufacturer would be:

Contact each current customer twice and make a sales presentation to the top 50 percent of prospect companies in the newly developed construction and manufacturing SIC target markets.

Make full product demonstrations to 75 percent of the prospects.

Obtain a sales ratio of 85 percent among existing customers and 30 percent among new prospects.

Obtain an average dollar sales of $2,500 and generate an average of 200 sales per salesperson per year.

Step 2: Establish Selling/Operations Strategies

It will be helpful first to review the questions in Step 7, Distribution, of the business review pertaining to selling. These will help you to form specific selling strategies for your company. In addition, the areas to address when you establish specific selling/operations strategies to meet your selling/operations objectives follow.

- *The type of selling environment.* A retailer must decide whether the selling environment will be self-service, or whether there will be a full-service sales staff. If there is a full-service sales staff, the decision must be made as to the selling orientation—hard sell or soft sell. A manufacturer must determine whether to use a direct, indirect, or mixed sales staff.

- *The administration parameters of the sales force.* The selling strategies should outline hiring qualifications, salary ranges, payment methods (annual salary, commissions, combination salary and commissions), training, and evaluation procedures.

- *Sales incentives.* If they will be used, sales incentive programs should be developed in this section of the plan.

- *Seasonal and geographic requirements.* If staffing is a function of seasonal sales or there are different staffing requirements by store or by market, there should be a selling strategy developed to address these issues.

- *Operational requirements.* The selling strategy section should also direct selling technique. For retailers, is there a certain selling technique that should be followed to increase the chance of closing a sale? A shoe retailer may require that its sales force initiate as many trial fittings as possible. This might result from data that shows fitting customers and allowing them to try walking in the shoe leads to a 25 percent higher sales ratio. Similar selling technique decisions should be considered for manufacturers.

- *Store operation guidelines.* Selling and operation strategies should cover stocking procedures; maintenance considerations; appearance of the store for retailers, the office for service, and shelf display for manufacturers; and product presentation in-store for retailers, in the office for service, and display of product for manufacturers.

- *The method of selling the product to intermediate markets.* A manufacturer must decide to sell direct (in-house sales force), indirect (through independant sales reps or brokers), or through a combination of the two.

The following are examples of selling strategies for a ski retailer whose selling objectives were to increase the sales ratio from 30 percent to 45 percent during the next year and to obtain a 35 percent ski equipment demonstration ratio among customers in the store.

Strategies

Develop an aggressive selling environment designed to sell customers during a one-on-one sales presentation in-store.

Develop a program assuring that all customers are greeted upon entry to the store.

Utilize the training hill outside the store as a means to get customers to actually try the equipment and achieve the demonstration goals established in the selling objectives.

Utilize two percent commission plus salary to encourage aggressive salespeople.

Establish a bonus system to reward the top producers each week and each month of the year.

Utilize mystery shoppers to rate service and selling effectiveness. Rate each salesperson at least once every six months.

Utilize annual and semi-annual reviews of the sales staff to improve performance. Send each salesperson to one selling seminar per year.

Develop quarterly seminars to keep salespeople aware of the latest technology and products in the industry.

Worksheet 11.1   Personal Selling/Operations

Selling/Operations Objectives

Selling/Operations Strategies

Rationale

Promotion

Promotion is a powerful short-term marketing tool. Developing a promotional plan requires strategic thinking and creativity. In many instances, marketers begin at the execution stage and randomly consider idea after idea without any thought as to the ends they are trying to achieve. The result is usually costly, with time and effort spent on developing promotion ideas that are inappropriate to the current market and the competitive situation. The key is to establish promotion objectives and strategies first and then develop innovative, yet *targeted,* executions.

DEFINITION

For the purposes of this book, we will define promotion as an activity offering added incentive to stimulate incremental purchase or association with the product over the short run, for a reason other than the product's inherent attributes and benefits. Promotion provides added incentive, encouraging the target market to perform some incremental behavior. The incremental behavior results in either increased short-term sales or an association with the product (e.g., product usage or an event oriented experience), or both. In addition, promotion is more short term in focus.

HOW TO DEVELOP PROMOTION OBJECTIVES

Promotion Objective Parameters

A worksheet for developing your promotion objectives is provided at the end of the chapter.

Promotion objectives and marketing objectives are very similar in that both are designed to affect consumer behavior. The difference is that promotion objectives should be designed to affect *specific incremental* behavior over a *short period of time.* Therefore, promotion objectives must:

- *Induce incremental consumer behavior over what was anticipated with no promotion.*

- *Be specific.* The objective should focus on one singular goal.

- *Be measurable.* The results must be able to be quantified.

- *Relate to a specific time period.* However, because promotion objectives are short term in nature, the time period can be from one day to several months.

- *Provide direction as to the geographical focus of the promotion.*

- *Include budget constraints or profit parameters.* This is because promotion is a marketing mix tool with its own sales objectives.

- *Focus on affecting target market behavior.* For example, the promotion should retain current users, increase purchases from current users, increase trial from new users, or obtain repeat usage after initial trial.

Promotions should be viewed as one method to help execute marketing strategies. In order to develop promotion objectives, you must first review the marketing objective and strategy section of your marketing plan and then restate your marketing strategies in quantifiable promotion objectives.

Step 1: Review Your Marketing Strategies

Review your marketing strategies, paying particular attention to those listed under the promotion category and those for which the implementation tool of promotion might be appropriate. A *marketing seasonality strategy,* such as increase sales during the weaker selling months of May through August, could be implemented through promotion. And, obviously, a *marketing promotion strategy,* such as develop in-store promotions during peak selling seasons to encourage purchases of weaker selling product categories, should be addressed in the promotional plan. Thus, the first step requires isolating those marketing strategies you feel promotions can help implement.

Step 2: Review the Selected Marketing Strategies and Their Corresponding Marketing Objectives

This step involves reviewing each marketing strategy selected to be implemented through promotions in Step 1 and its corresponding marketing objective. In order to form promotion objectives, the marketer reviews the marketing objective to determine *what* needs to be accomplished and *who* is being targeted. Then rely on your marketing strategy to guide you on *how* to develop a promotion objective. By linking your promotion objective to your marketing objective and strategy, you ensure greater probability of developing promotions that will accomplish your marketing strategies and fulfill the marketing objectives established earlier in the plan. Assume the following situation:

Marketing Objective: Increase the number of total users among the current target market by 10 percent.

Seasonality Marketing Strategy: Increase the purchasing level during the off-season, while maintaining purchasing rates during the peak selling seasons.

Note that there would typically be other marketing strategies to achieve the above marketing objective. However, assume that only the seasonality strategy is being implemented through promotion, and the other marketing strategies would be accomplished using other marketing mix executional tools. In this example, the *marketing objective* will provide *what* the promotion objective should achieve and *whom* the promotion should target.

Increase number of users (marketing goal, *what*).

From the current target market (target market goal, *who*).

Continuing, the *market strategy* will help determine *how* the promotion objective is developed.

Increase purchasing during the off-season (method of achievement, *how*).

Step 3: Restate the What, Who, and How Portions in a Quantifiable Promotion Objective

In combining what, who, and how, the marketing objective and strategy can be restated into a quantifiable promotion objective as follows:

Increase the number of users from the current target market by 25 percent during the off-season of May and June in all markets, with a positive contribution to overhead.

Note that *geography* and *timing* considerations and a *measurable amount* are incorporated into the objective statement to make it as specific as possible. Geography and timing in the promotion objective would be consistent with the geography and timing constraints developed in the marketing strategy section of the plan. Also, note that a budget constraint is mentioned. In this case, the objective has to be achieved in a manner that contributes positively to fixed overhead. Yet, in a different situation, the objective of new trial might outweigh any short-term profit requirement because the company would be investing in new customers or trial for future profits. However, there would be a budget constraint at the end of the promotion objective to limit the amount of the investment in new trial. The promotion objective might be "increase the number of new users by 25 percent during the off-season with a promotion budget not to exceed $500,000." The budget constraint serves to tailor the promotion execution by providing a parameter for how much new trial is required.

The measurable amount in the promotion objective (in this example, 25 percent) must be realistic. Past experience provides the best assistance in deciding just how much you will affect target market behavior through promotions. Remember that promotion is just one marketing tool you will be using to achieve your marketing objectives. If promotions were the only implementation tool, then the measurable goal in the promotion objective would have to equal the measurable goal in the marketing objective. In this example, the goal would have to be to add enough incremental new users during May and June to increase the total new user base for the year 10 percent above last year's results. This is highly unrealistic and points out why there are usually multiple marketing strategies for any given marketing objective. In addition, promotion is most often only *partially* responsible for the implementation of any given marketing strategy. Other marketing tools, such as advertising, distribution, pricing, and merchandising, might also be used in conjunction with promotion to implement a specific marketing strategy.

In going through the above process, you may develop several promotion objectives, as there may be several marketing strategies that can be implemented and accomplished through the use of promotions. Each promotion objective will require one or more promotional strategies.

PROMOTION STRATEGY AND EXECUTION CONSIDERATIONS

Promotion Strategy Parameters

Once the promotional objectives are established, promotion strategies must be formulated demonstrating how to accomplish the promotion objectives. Promotion strategies should include:

- Type of promotion device
- The promotion incentive
- Whether to implement a closed or open promotion
- The delivery method

Type of Promotion Device

The marketer has to determine which promotional device (price off/sale, couponing, sampling, on pack/in pack, refunds, premiums, sweepstakes/ games, packaging, trade allowances, events) will best meet the promotion objective.

The Promotion Incentive

The promotion incentive must include a *basic reward* for the consumer. Since promotions are responsible for affecting target market behavior, the incentive must stimulate demand. The promotion incentive must be strong enough to move the market to participate in the promotion and purchase the product.

Closed versus Open Promotions

A promotion can be open or closed. There are also degrees between these two extremes. An *open promotion* is one where the company offers an added incentive to purchase with no specific behavior required to take advantage of the offer. A good example of this would be a 20 percent off sale at the retail level. In order to take advantage of this incentive or offer, consumers merely have to shop at the store. Anyone can participate, with no restrictions.

With a *closed promotion,* an added incentive to purchase is offered to consumers, but they are required to do something in order to take advantage of the offer. An example would be a coupon that must be redeemed at purchase or a refund that requires ten proof-of-purchase validations.

There are degrees to the extent that a promotion is open or closed. Consider the example of instant coupons: the requirement of the individual consumer, beyond simply shopping, is minimal. The customer has to tear a coupon off the package and present it at the checkout counter. However, a promotion such as a refund requiring multiple proofs-of-purchase may prove to be very restrictive. This type of promotion requires a great deal of consumer purchase commitment before the incentive is received.

Delivery Method

Promotions can be delivered by three basic methods or a combination thereof:

- *Media.* There are multiple forms of media delivered promotions. Direct mail, magazines, and newspapers are the most common media delivery methods for package goods and business-to-business firms, while television, newspaper, direct mail, and radio are the most common media delivery methods for retail firms.

- *On, in, or near package.* For manufacturers, promotions can be delivered on the package itself, in the package, or near the package via a point-of-purchase display. For retailers, the promotions can be delivered in-store through signage and point-of-purchase displays.

- *Salespeople.* Many companies, especially manufacturers, such as package goods or business-to-business firms that sell to intermediate markets, use salespeople to deliver a promotional offer. If the target market is not a major consumer group but a more limited purchasing group, direct personal communication of an offer can be efficient and very effective.

HOW TO DEVELOP PROMOTION STRATEGIES AND PROGRAMS

Now comes the fun part. The process of actually establishing promotion strategies is fairly simple and allows for a great deal of creative flexibility. A worksheet is provided at the end of the chapter.

Step 1: Review Your Promotion Objectives

Review your promotion objectives to make certain you are focused on what you are trying to accomplish. Be particularly cognizant of who you are targeting and the measurable result that is expected.

Step 2: Review Your Problems and Opportunities

Review the listing of your problems and opportunities, as these are your knowledge base and will provide insights and ideas on what direction you should pursue in developing your promotion strategies. As you are reviewing your problems and opportunities, refer to your idea page (discussed in the introduction to this book), where you can write down any ideas you may have. Refer to this later when you are actually formulating your strategies.

Two purchase rate/buying habit problems might be:

The average shopper is extremely brand loyal.

The Southwest consumes the product category at below average rates on a per capita basis, and your company has poor sales in this region of the country.

These two problems will affect your promotional strategies in the area of what incentive to offer. Knowing that the category is extremely brand loyal means that it will be very difficult to induce trial, so the incentive will have to be greater. And if you are going to target the Southwest, the challenge will be even greater, since it is a low consumption area where your company has poor sales.

These are examples of how your problems and opportunities will provide direction and insights concerning development of your promotion strategies. Study your problems and opportunities very carefully. They will help you in developing intelligent, databased promotion strategies.

Step 3: Finalize Your Promotion Strategies

A promotion strategy must incorporate each of the issues outlined in the section on strategy parameters:

- Type of promotion device
- Promotion incentive
- Closed or open promotion
- Delivery method

Assume the following situation:

Marketing Objective: Increase usage rates among the target market nationally over the next year by 20 percent.

Marketing Strategy: Expand alternative uses of the product from exclusively a hot drink to include acceptance as a cold beverage.

Promotion Objective: Obtain initial trial of 100,000 new customers nationally for the product as a cold beverage during the months of April and May. Achieve initial trial with a budget of $2,000,000.

Note that with this situation there would probably be an alternative promotion objective aimed at stimulating trial from among the existing customer base. This objective would have separate promotion strategies and executions.

The following promotion strategies could be utilized to accomplish the promotion objective. Each of four strategy parameters will be addressed.

The cost parameter is addressed only indirectly through the choice of an incentive amount. It will be covered in more detail in Step 5.

Promotional Strategy Examples

Utilize sampling of the product in-store to soft drink purchasers.

Provide coupons to potential customers in-store worth 50 cents off the purchase price the day of the sampling.

Incorporate a trade program offering price incentives as a way to induce shelf space and merchandising support.

Step 4: Develop Alternative Promotion Program Executions

The next step is to develop alternative executions for each promotion strategy. Then choose the most appropriate execution for inclusion in your program. Multiple executions can be developed for each promotion strategy. Be creative and think of as many as you can. Some alternative promotion executions are presented in Exhibit 12.1. These alternatives were developed to meet two of the strategies: "Utilize sampling of the product in-store," and "Provide 50-cent coupons to potential customers in-store." A worksheet to help you channel your thinking and stay consistent from one execution to another is provided at the end of this chapter.

Note that there is a sales objective included. Since promotions are a short-term marketing tool affecting customer behavior, there will be short-term sales results generated by the promotion. Thus it is a good idea to establish a sales goal along with the promotion objectives, strategies, and executions. Then when you analyze your promotion results, you will have two results to gauge your success against—the sales goal and the quantitative promotion objective.

Step 5: Calculate the Cost and Payback Potential of Your Promotions

Expenses must be projected for each promotion in your promotional plan. Included should be all costs associated with communicating and delivering the promotion to the target market. This includes media costs associated with delivering the promotion. (This does *not* include the media costs associated with your normal nonpromotion/image advertising.) In addition, you must also estimate the cost of the offer or incentive. If you use 25-cent coupons, you must estimate the redemption number and multiply this by 25 cents plus handling costs to calculate a dollar cost of the coupon incentive.

Cost Calculation for Closed Promotion

In order to calculate the cost and potential payback of closed promotions, you need to accurately project participation of redemption rates for your offer. A worksheet is provided at the end of the chapter. The following will provide you with ballpark estimates for participation or redemption rates using different closed promotion vehicles. Actual participation rates should be individually adjusted because they are a function of the following:

EXHIBIT 12.1 Alternative Promotion Program Execution

Program Theme

"Have one on us."

Sales Objective

Develop sales of $20,000,000 over a two-month period.

Promotion Objective

Obtain initial trial of 100,000 new customers nationally for the product as a cold beverage during the months of April and May. Achieve the initial trial with a budget of $2,000,000.

Promotion Strategies

Utilize sampling of the product in-store to soft drink purchasers.

Provide coupons to potential customers in-store worth 50 cents off the purchase price wherever the product is sampled.

Description

Display a giant, self-serve beverage bottle with product being served hot from one side and cold from the other in grocery stores carrying the product.

Offer free samples in paper cups to all shoppers during four weeks in April and May, effectively leading the summer selling period.

Provide a 50-cent instant coupon to all customers who sample the product.

Support

In-store signage and display.

Rationale

The promotion will build trial and exposure for the new cold drink. Serving the cold drink with the established hot drink will show customers alternative uses for the product and link the new brand to an established and accepted product. April and May were chosen as the time to sample because the time period effectively bridges cold and warm weather months.

The instant coupon will encourage immediate purchase after trial. The 50-cent incentive will be a strong inducement and, along with the sampling, will lower the risk of trying an unknown product.

Note: Alternative executions would be developed for the same objectives and strategies. You could then choose the execution that most effectively and efficiently meets the objectives.

- *The offer*—greater incentive and fewer restrictions equals greater participation.

- *The product category*—for example, health and beauty aids have average redemption rates lower than those of household products or beverages.

- *Total cost of product*—the higher the cost of the product, the less the participation.

The participation estimates shown in Exhibit 12.2 are based on a combination of our client experience and redemption averages published by industry sources.

Exhibit 12.3 demonstrates how to calculate the cost of a promotion. A worksheet is provided at the end of this chapter. We used a coupon promotion

EXHIBIT 12.2 Estimated Participation and Redemption Rates

Promotion Technique	Average Redemption Range	
	Low	High
Newspaper (run of paper—ROP)	0.5%	3.5%
Newspaper co-op (multiple coupons from different companies in one promotion piece)	0.8	3.4
Free standing insert (FSI)	2.5	6.0
Magazine on page	0.8	2.6
Magazine pop up	2.5	6.5
Direct mail	0.5	10.0
In product	10.0	15.0
On product	8.0	12.0
Cross-ruff or cross-pack	4.0	8.0
Self-liquidating point-of-sales premium	0.3	1.0
Refunds	0.5	3.5
Instant coupon on pack	15.0	25.0

EXHIBIT 12.3 Calculating Cost of a Coupon Promotion

	High	Medium	Low
Redemption Costs			
Value of coupon	50¢	50¢	50¢
Number of coupons distributed	500,000	500,000	500,000
Estimated redemption rate	4.0%	2.0%	0.5%
Number redeemed	20,000	10,000	2,500
Dollar value or offer (number redeemed x value of coupon)	$10,000	$5,000	$1,250
Advertising and Media Costs			
Printing of coupons (500,000 x 0.01)	$ 5,000	$ 5,000	$ 5,000
Mailing cost/envelopes (500,000 x 0.19)	95,000	95,000	95,000
Total cost of promotion	$110,000	$105,000	$101,250

as an example because it has applications to retail, package goods, and business-to-business firms. Three different redemption rates were used to provide the marketer with a range of expected responses. The cost of this promotion would be somewhere between $110,000 and $101,250, with a medium estimate of $105,000. This cost will be used along with incremental sales and profits when calculating potential payback for a closed promotion.

In addition, if you are a package goods firm with coupon redemption in grocery stores, there are handling charges to be included. If you are utilizing a clearinghouse, you must pay a charge for each coupon handled. Also, the grocer charges for each coupon handled. At press time of this book, the average total cost was approximately 10 to 12 cents per coupon redeemed.

Finally, the cost of the promotion must be compared to the incremental sales the promotion is expected to generate. This can be determined through a payback analysis.

Payback Analysis

Before you execute any planned promotion, you should make sure to review the numbers to determine whether the promotion makes sense from a payback analysis standpoint. We recommend calculating the contribution to fixed costs,[1] as this method isolates the promotion and takes into account any incremental variable cost associated with the promotion. In using this method, incremental costs of the promotion (communication of the promotion and incentive costs) are subtracted from incremental sales generated from the promotion.

Exhibit 12.4 presents an example for a retailer considering a 20 percent off sale as an open promotion. A worksheet is provided at the end of this chapter. The retailer had experience with similar sales in the past and had a rough estimate on the incremental sales that could be generated by the promotional offer. This method looks at incremental sales and costs to calculate what the promotion will generate in terms of a contribution to fixed overhead. The incremental margin sales are sales above and beyond what would normally be expected for the time period. In this case, the retailer had a good idea of what to expect. If you haven't run the promotion before, make a high,

EXHIBIT 12.4   Payback Calculation Example for Open Promotion

Situation
Promotion: 20 percent off women's department merchandise.
Estimated storewide margin decrease from 50 percent to 45 percent during promotion.
Time period: First three weeks of March.
Geography: All three stores in Madison, WI.

Sales

Estimated sales for period without promotion	$300,000
Estimated gross margin dollars for period without promotion ($300,00 x .50)	150,000
Estimated sales with promotion	360,000
Estimated gross margin dollars with promotion ($360,000 x .45)	162,000
Estimated net margin dollar increase with promotion ($162,000 – $150,000)	12,000

Media and Advertising Cost

Estimated ongoing advertising and media costs with or without promotion*	15,000
Total advertising and media costs with promotion	20,000
Incremental advertising and media costs due to promotion	5,000

Payout

Incremental margin sales	12,000
Incremental advertising and media expenditures	5,000
Contribution to fixed overhead	7,000

*What would have been spent in regular mainline advertising and media.

---

[1]This method is commonly used by retailers, service firms, and manufacturers. However, manufacturers also utilize a gross margin for net sales method detailed in Chapter 17, Marketing Budget, Payback Analysis, and Marketing Calendar.

medium, and low estimate based on similar promotions in the past. This provides best, most likely, and worst case estimates.

Note that the *cost of the promotion* (reduction in gross margin dollars) was calculated directly into the projected incremental sales figure. In some cases, you may want to break this step out to show what the promotion costs were, particularly if you are a package goods marketer and you wish to show redemption projections.

Remember, the promotion must stand on its own. The only way to determine its potential success or failure is to weigh the projected incremental sales against the expected incremental expenses of the promotion. If the promotion contributes a meaningful positive dollar figure to fixed overhead (expenses that occur no matter what happens, e.g., rent) and meets the promotion sales goals, then the promotion should be executed. If the payback analysis shows that there is a negative contribution to fixed overhead, then you should consider another promotion, or rework the promotion with less incentive or a different product mix. The exception to this is if there is no budget parameter specifying that the promotion must contribute to profits. If the firm is simply trying to gain trial, which it believes will translate into future profits, then the major constraints will be the budget parameter and the amount of desired trial.

Step 6: Select the Most Appropriate Promotion Executions

You have developed promotion objectives and strategies, created promotion execution alternatives, and analyzed costs and paybacks for each execution. Now it is time to select those executions that will best achieve the promotion objectives within the budget constraints established. When choosing your promotion executions, try to make sure the executions complement each other and work together through the year. Two premium offers back-to-back would probably be ineffective compared to other combinations of promotions. The best method to determine whether your promotions properly interface with each other is to list the promotions in calendar form according to when they will be executed. This will allow you to judge whether you have selected promotions that complement each other. It will also be useful when you are transferring your marketing tool executions to one master calendar as is detailed in Chapter 17, Marketing Budget, Payback Analysis, and Marketing Calendar.

Worksheet 12.1   Promotion

Promotion Objectives

Promotion Strategies

Rationale

Worksheet 12.2   Promotion Program Execution

Program Theme

Sales Objective

Promotion Objective

Promotion Strategies

Description

Support

Rationale

Worksheet 12.3

Calculating Cost of a Coupon Promotion

	High	Medium	Low

Redemption Costs

Value of coupon

Number of coupons distributed

Estimated redemption rate

Number redeemed

Dollar value or offer (number redeemed
   x value of coupon)

Advertising and Media Costs

Printing of coupons

Mailing cost/envelopes

   Total cost of promotion

Worksheet 12.4   Payback Calculation for Open Promotion

Situation
Promotion:
Time period:
Geography:

Sales
Estimated sales for period without promotion
Estimated gross margin dollars for period without promotion
Estimated sales with promotion
Estimated gross margin dollars with promotion
Estimated net margin dollar increase with promotion

Media and Advertising Cost
Estimated ongoing advertising and media costs with or without promotion*
Total advertising and media costs with promotion
Incremental advertising and media costs due to promotion

Payout
Incremental margin sales
Incremental advertising and media expenditures
Contribution to fixed overhead

---

*What would have been spent in regular mainline advertising and media.

Advertising Message

Now that you have decided how to market, position, price, distribute, sell, and promote your product, you are ready to write the advertising message segment of your marketing plan. This is another key learning chapter because it deals with the translation of marketing into advertising, which is usually the most visible communication to your external and internal targets.

DEFINITION

Before discussing how the communication elements are factored into a marketing plan, it is necessary to understand what advertising really is versus the other communication elements. It is a common error to bunch advertising, public relations or publicity, promotion, and merchandising together as one and the same. In fact, all these forms of communication are very different from each other in terms of what they are capable of doing and what role they each play in the marketing plan. For this marketing plan discussion, we will define advertising as that which informs and persuades through *paid* media (television, radio, magazine, newspaper, outdoor, and direct mail) .

THE DISCIPLINED PROCESS FOR ADVERTISING

Because of its tremendous attention getting power and inherent creativity, advertising is continuously on stage for everyone to critique. Accordingly, nearly everyone thinks he or she is an expert on advertising because it is a subjective marketing tool. Therefore, it stands to reason that the more subjective it is as a marketing tool, the more necessary it is to use a disciplined process to arrive at advertising that sells. This is basically a 1-2-3 process:

1. Define your advertising objectives.

2. Write your advertising strategy.

3. Detail what will go into the execution.

No doubt by now you have come up with a number of advertising ideas. However, before going ahead and actually executing your creative ideas, go through this disciplined process. Using this disciplined approach will assure that the final advertising will be effective, or at least more effective than if you had gone with the first ad idea that came to mind. Also, it should be pointed out that your market positioning is the key to effective advertising. It is in essence the bridge from the more objective marketing to the more subjective advertising.

Step 1: Advertising Objectives
Advertising Awareness and Attitude Objectives

Advertising objectives deal with what you want your advertising to accomplish. Your advertising objectives nearly always will define awareness and attitude goals as they relate to the target market. The objectives are quantifiable, while the advertising strategy is not. The strategy deals primarily with describing the necessary message communication to fulfill the advertising objectives.

At the minimum, to help sell the product, advertising must first attract attention, building awareness for your product. While just having awareness will help sell some product, in most cases the target market must also have a positive attitude toward what you are selling, particularly beyond what is being marketed by the competition.

Before you begin to set your objectives, check that you did *not* include advertising objectives in your marketing objectives and strategies section. The tendency is to deal with such communication issues as recall and understanding under marketing, but they belong under advertising.

Measurable Advertising Objectives

The foundation for setting advertising objectives is the fact that awareness leads to an attitude formation, which leads to behavior. In most purchase situations, you can't have an increase in purchase behavior until there has been a positive shift in attitudes about your product. And increase in awareness of your product and its communication is a prerequisite for shifts in attitudes. Therefore, advertising objectives focus on increasing awareness and establishing positive purchase attributes as determined by the target market.

Awareness measures can be quantified by determining the percentage of the target market that is aware of your product or company and then establishing increases in awareness the coming year. This is accomplished through primary research. Over time, you will be able to develop historical norms to help you to predict how increases in awareness translate to increases in active behavior (purchases and sales).

Attitude measures can be quantified by establishing goals for attitudinal shifts across key purchase attributes. For example, if value is the most important target market purchase variable, you need to monitor shifts in the perception of your product in terms of value.

When setting the advertising objectives, remember to make them measurable. Even if you are not planning or cannot afford to implement a research program to measure the effectiveness of the advertising, setting measurable advertising objectives will force you to objectively evaluate the advertising challenge. Further, if your time period to achieve the advertising objectives differs from the time period set for the marketing objectives, indicate the time period with the advertising objectives.

The following example shows how to define your advertising objectives. It is easier to set your advertising objectives if you have primary research. However, in many cases you will not have done market research that establishes a benchmark from which to measure awareness and attitude changes. Nevertheless, it is a good learning process to estimate (even if you can only make educated guesses) what percentage of unaided awareness is necessary to affect a predisposed attitude to buy that then translates to a specific percentage of the target market that will purchase. Now you can relate this purchase number back to your marketing objective.

	Percent	Number
Total target market	100%	100,000
Unaided awareness	40	40,000
Probably/definitely will purchase	10	10,000
Purchasers	5	5,000

Examples of Advertising Objectives

Awareness Objectives

Increase unaided awareness among the target market from 18 percent to 25 percent.

Establish among the target market an unaided awareness percentage twice that of the product's current share of market.

Attitudinal Objectives

Move the product quality attitude ranking among the target market from fourth to third place.

Establish a leadership image with 25 percent of the target market.

Step 2: Advertising Strategy

The advertising strategy, also referred to as the creative strategy, is the catalyst of effective advertising. It provides direction on what should be communicated in the advertising message and how it should be communicated. It is a big part of the means that gets the desired product perception into the mind of the consumer. This strategy is the guide for development of creative and communicative advertising in order to gain attention, be remembered, positively affect attitudes, and help move the target market to purchase your product. It becomes a guide for those (possibly yourself) who will actually create the advertising. Further, the advertising strategy describes the personality of the advertising and the parameters of the creative environment in which the advertising must perform. Without this guide, the final advertising could very well be exceptionally entertaining but not necessarily effective. Although you may like the advertising, it might not communicate the benefits of the product that will fulfill the needs and wants of the specified target market.

The advertising strategy is not only a guide for creative development but also the basis against which creative work is evaluated to make sure that advertising communicates effectively. Usually you want to develop alternative creative approaches (copy, layout, storyboards, etc.) against the agreed upon advertising strategy and then judge the best approach to execute the strategy. Also, if you are having an advertising agency execute the creative, both the client and the agency should contribute and mutually agree to the written strategy before it is executed. This strategy agreement is necessary so that when the advertising work is presented, there is no confusion or disagreement in terms of the description of the product, specific benefits, claims made, and feeling of the advertising. Further, having an agreed upon strategy up front will save time in creative development and help eliminate frustration for all involved.

The advertising strategy should include the following:

- *Promise:* Define the reward/benefit for the target market in solving a problem or taking advantage of an opportunity.

- *Support for This Promise:* Give substantiation for the promise or reasons to believe.

- *Tone:* Describe the feeling of the planned advertising that is consistent with the personality of the product. The tone must be appropriate not only for your product but also for the target market of the advertising.

Look to your positioning statement for direction in writing the advertising strategy, because it will be the key in developing an advertising strategy to differentiate your product from the competition. Make sure your advertising strategy speaks directly to conveying the image you want to instill in the minds of the target market.

Don't expect to complete an advertising strategy on the first attempt. Plan to rewrite each segment of the advertising strategy a number of times until you arrive at a strategy that clearly states what you want your final advertising to communicate. Each word in your advertising strategy is critical; therefore, make sure it communicates the intended meaning. However, do not expect to see a *lift* of the strategy wording in the finished advertising. Keep the strategy simple for clarity and single minded for focus. Make sure your strategy conveys the inherent personality of your product that can come alive in your advertising.

The advertising strategy that has been reworked and included in your marketing plan should be the strategy that reflects the positioning and provides the overall direction for a unified advertising campaign. However, it might be that your marketing plan calls for additional but separate advertising strategies, such as for specific products within a company line. An advertising strategy for Green Giant Corn would be a modification of the overall campaign strategy for Green Giant Canned Vegetables. Or you may need separate strategies for special geographic and demographic markets, promotions, or trade advertising.

Although it is likely you will need substrategies, it is important that your overall advertising strategy is written to be a *campaign strategy to guide all your advertising*: consumer and/or business-to-business, promotional and institutional, and subset geographic or demographic targets. Your primary strategy should lead to an advertising campaign in which all the individual advertisements continually reinforce your positioning. This is vital, because an advertising campaign will create a unified image and will provide a consistency for all your creative executions. Obviously, there are always exceptions to this, particularly if you are marketing very different products to very different target markets.

An effective selling, strategic advertising campaign will incorporate similarities. The advertising within a campaign should include as many common properties as possible, such as a similar look, sound, and feel or tonality that conveys a consistent personality. Further, in most cases, each advertisement will include a unified basic selling idea (theme line) such as "Fly the Friendly Skies" or "Marlboro Country."

The rewards of developing a campaign are many. It will become cumulative in scope, with each advertisement reinforcing the others for a multiple effect, making your advertising work harder and maximizing your advertising investment.

The following presents an example of how to write an advertising strategy for a hospital marketing its obstetrics department. Worksheets for the advertising objectives and message strategy are provided at the end of this chapter.

Promise

Convince the married woman age 18 to 34 that General Hospital is the special place to give birth to her child because it is the only hospital that provides both the best personal and professional care for baby and mother.

Support for This Promise

Mothers have rated General Hospital's OB Department the best in providing personal care when having a baby, and it has been officially designated as the area's referral hospital for high risk expectant mothers and newborn babies.

Tone of the Advertising

The tone of the advertising will be preemptive and professional but personal, conveying a warm and enduring feeling consistent with individual care and safety provided to baby and mother.

Step 3: Consider the Executional Elements

The execution portion of your advertising section outlines those specifics that must be included in the advertising. Under executional considerations, you might want to include additional copy or product information that is important to know but, to maintain strategic focus, is not included in the advertising strategy. This additional product information will provide for creative enhancement and increased understanding when developing the actual advertising.

Another executional consideration is the legality of the advertising. Make sure everything you include in the advertising is truthful and can be documented. In this section or in a separate implementation plan, list any legal restrictions/considerations you are aware of for your product, the target market, and the geographic area that will receive the advertising.

Along with legal considerations (if not included in a separate implementation plan), list any advertising requirements. For example:

- How the company and product name/logo must be used in the advertising

- How the theme line must be used in all advertising

- Product line/store locations to be included

- Preproduction copy test requirements, production cost parameters, ad size, etc.

Most often the executional considerations of the advertising section are not included in the marketing plan but are detailed in what is sometimes called an advertising implementation plan. This plan includes all the information necessary for those responsible to create the advertising.

The following presents an example of items in the advertising executional considerations section. Worksheets to use for preparing the advertising message and for implementing the advertising plan are provided at the end of this chapter.

Additional/Key Strategy Information

More babies have been delivered at General Hospital than any other hospital in the area.

General Hospital has the most experienced physician and nursing staff.

Specific Legal Considerations

Include title of research study as disclaimer in the advertising as support for superiority claim.

Advertising Requirements

Include advertising theme "We care . . . A lot" in all advertising.

List both site locations in all advertising.

Worksheet 13.1   Advertising Message

Objectives

Awareness

Attitudes

Rationale for Objectives

Advertising Strategy

Promise

Support for this Promise

Tone of the Advertising

Worksheet 13.1 Advertising Message (Continued)

Rationale for Strategy

Advertising Execution Considerations
(If no separate advertising implementation plan is prepared)

Additional/Key Strategy Information

Specific Legal Considerations

Advertising Requirements

Advertising Media

Now that you understand the promotional and image messages to be externally communicated, the next step is to prepare a media plan that will most effectively and efficiently deliver these messages. You will find that learning how to plan media is one of the most challenging, complex experiences you will encounter as you write your marketing plan.

DEFINITION

Media can be divided into two parts: planning and execution. The overall goal of media planning and execution is to deliver the optimum number of impressions (messages) to the target audience at the lowest cost within the most suitable environment for the message.

Planning consists of arranging the various media in combinations and support levels designed to most effectively and efficiently fulfill the marketing, advertising, and promotion objectives and strategies. It is in essence the process of refining probabilities in a step-by-step, disciplined manner.

Execution, on the other hand, encompasses negotiating, purchasing, and placing the media once the media weights, types, and budgets have been determined. Another part of media execution is the evaluation of the purchased media's performance once it has run. This chapter concentrates only on media planning. Refer to a text on media buying if you intend to purchase your own media.

The actual media plan included in the marketing plan consists of three basic elements:

- Media objectives

- Media strategies

- Media plan calendar and budget summary

THE DISCIPLINED APPROACH TO MEDIA PLANNING

Step 1: Review Information Needed to Write a Media Plan

Before you can begin to prepare your media plan, you must first review all the pertinent marketing and media data. Most of this information should be included in your business review. Below is a list of marketing and media data to be reviewed over a three-to-five-year period, with five years of history preferred. Attempt to gather and review all of the items, depending on the data and time available to you.

- Review the size and growth of the marketplace in dollars and units.

- Analyze the competitive market (including your product):

  If available, state sales history of each major competitor by size, share, and growth.

  If available, review competitive media for each major competitor:

  > Level and share of media spending/weight

  > Spending and weight levels by medium, seasonality (quarterly if possible), and market

  > Media spending as a percent of sales

  If available, review unaided awareness, advertising awareness, and attitudes of the potential users/purchasers, on both a national/systemwide and market-by-market basis.

- Analyze your product's sales, marketing, and media history.

  State sales history by product, market, and store/distribution channel.

  State your media target market.

  If available, review unaided awareness, advertising awareness, attitudes, and behavior/usage.

  Give a historical media review of your product:

  > Overall media weight delivery and spending

  > Spending and weight levels by medium (quarterly) and market

  > Media spending as percent of sales

  List results of media schedules run:

  > Changes in awareness, attitudes, and behavior

  > Impact on overall sales, promotions, events, and media tests

  Review the dollars allocated to media versus the other marketing mix tools.

- Review the problems and opportunities section.

- Review this marketing plan again, from sales objectives through advertising message. This information will point out what the media plan must accomplish and provide direction for the development of the media plan.

Step 2: Set the Media Objectives

Your media objectives must provide a clear and definitive direction in the following critical areas.

- To whom the advertising is to be directed (target audience)

- Where the advertising is to go (geography)

- When the advertising is to appear (seasonality)

- How much advertising is deemed sufficient to achieve the advertising objectives (media weight levels)

- Determination of whether there is a going-in set budget allocated for media spending or if a task method approach will be applied to arrive at a media budget. If there is a set going-in media budget allocation, it should be included up front in the media plan as a media objective. A task derived media budget is dependent on the media support necessary to meet the awareness and attitude levels that will stimulate adequate usage to meet the sales objectives. In this case, the media budget is finalized and presented at the end of the media plan.

Target Audience

To arrive at a target audience, simplify the target market you have already detailed by listing the key strategic and demographic descriptors. The *strategic target* relates to purchasing and usage. Mothers purchase powdered soft drinks for their children, and their children are the users. The *demographic target* audience should parallel the media demographic breakouts provided by syndicated media services that measure audience media habits and such media vendors as direct mail houses, broadcasting stations, and catalog publishers. If you have key submarkets, such as the trade (wholesalers, retailers, etc.) for a package good product, that cannot be accommodated in one media plan, a separate media plan should be prepared for them. The media target audience should be limited to those descriptors that can be readily and effectively used in the planning, measurement, and evaluation of the various media.

Some target audience examples for a CPA firm would be:

Companies that do not use a CPA firm;
Businesses with less than $3 million in revenues; and
The president, owner, and treasurer/financial officer

Target audience examples for a company selling hot dogs would be:

Heavy purchasers of hot dogs for the family,
Women age 18 to 49,
Households with incomes of $15,000–30,000, and
Households of three or more persons.

Geography

Once you have determined your specific media target audience, you must decide where and with what emphasis you want to place your media. Geographic media variation depends on the marketing strategies, as well as sales potential and profitability differences on a market-by-market basis or within a market. Geographic weighting of media levels by market is based on many factors. A number of these geographic factors to be considered when developing geography media objectives are:

- Sheer geographic size and physical makeup of your trading area
- Competitive media activity
- Media available to support your product
- Concentration of potential users of your product
- Concentration and trending of your product sales

In addition to the above considerations, you must also consider the trending of sales on a market-by-market basis. You might place additional media weight in markets with positive sales trends, while in markets with negative sales trends you might reduce the weight until a nonadvertising problem is fixed, or add media weight to support promotional advertising to reverse the sales trend.

Some examples for a business-to-business company would be:

To provide broad based media support of the full line of existing equipment, or

To provide full introductory media support in addition to base support of the East, North, and Central divisions for the new equipment introduction as soon as service commitment has been confirmed.

Some examples for a local retailer would be:

To provide marketwide media coverage, or

To provide incremental media weight within one mile of the store that accounts for 50 percent of current customers.

Seasonality

As important as it is to advertise to the right person in the right place, it is also important to advertise at the right time. Accordingly, to arrive at the right seasonality media objectives, you must review the seasonality of your product sales, as well as of the category, to determine when sales for your product and the category are at their highest levels. A normal media practice is to plan your greatest media weight support for periods of high sales volume.

Most products have sales skews. When monthly sales are higher than average, you would most likely heavy-up (increase) your weight levels. Sometimes the seasonality of your product might differ from that of the category, with the category's heavy sales season beginning earlier or later than that of your product. After reviewing the reasons for this seasonal sales difference (e.g., special promotion or different competitive weight levels), you will probably want to concentrate your media weight when the target market is most likely to purchase. However, you must still support with media a successful sales period that might have been self-created or when customers have been conditioned to purchase.

Another key point is to lead the natural buying season, placing higher levels of media just before and at the beginning of the heavier sales periods. Another factor to consider in setting a media seasonality objective is what the competition has done in the past and what you anticipate they will do in the coming year. You may want not only to lead the peak selling season but also to be the first into the media arena, preempting the competition.

An example of a seasonality objective for a local retailer would be to provide media continuity support throughout the year with a concentration of media effort in the heavy selling seasons of August to October and February to April.

Media Weight Goals

Having determined your media objectives of target audience, geography, and seasonality, you must next determine "how much is enough" in terms of the quantitative media delivery necessary to meet the awareness and attitude goals that will lead to projected sales.

Review of Rating Points, Reach, Frequency, and GRPs. Determining quantitative communications goals is very difficult even for the most experienced media planner because of the ever changing marketing environment in which there are no real definitive benchmarks, an uncontrollable competitive marketplace, and the continually changing needs and wants of the potential target market. Making it even more difficult is the problem of accurately determining how much communication is received by the target market and its effectiveness in stimulating action.

Before discussing how to arrive at quantitative communication goals to provide media direction, you must have an understanding of some basic media terms: rating point, GRPs (gross rating points), reach, and frequency. A *rating point is* defined as 1 percent of the universe being measured. A universe could include households, companies, women, men, adults, children, purchasing agents, etc., in a single market, region, or the total United States. On a total U.S. household basis, a one rating for a commercial or ad means an impression or exposure is made against approximately 940,000 homes nationally (1% of 94,000,000 homes). On a single market basis for Chicago, a one rating equates to approximately 31,000 homes (1% of 3,100,000 homes).

A *GRP* measures how much media weight is going into a defined marketplace and helps make comparisons among different media. When we buy 100 home GRPs via multiple ad insertions, we are in fact buying the number of homes equal to the total number of homes in that universe. Chicago has approximately 3,100,000 homes with 1 GRP = 31,000 homes and 100 GRPs = 3,100,000 homes. In actuality, when a schedule of ads or commercials is run, some of these homes will be reached more than once, and others not at all. Therefore, some people will see the ad a number of times and others will not see it at all, which leads to the following important media estimate terminology: *Reach* is how many different homes/persons we have reached (expressed as an absolute or %). *Frequency* is how often they have been reached on an average basis.

Reach expresses the number exposed at least once; frequency expresses the average number of exposures. GRPs, in the aggregate, represent the total magnitude of a schedule's exposures or a sum of the ratings. When the percent ratings of a specific market segment (example: Women age 18 +) are totaled, you have *target audience GRPs,* or, more simply stated, TRPs (target rating points). GRPs, a generic media term, may refer to household GRPs or specific target segment GRPs. A media schedule that delivers 80% reach with a 10 frequency against a specific market equals a total of 800 GRPs. Very simply:

Percent reach x Frequency = Total GRPs.

Normally we estimate reach and frequency on a four-week basis, but we can also provide reach and frequency for a weekly promotion, a total schedule, and on an annual basis.

Through research and experience, we have been able to establish standard reach levels for given GRP levels. Using the graph in Exhibit 14.1, you can determine what each medium should generate in reach or GRPs, and you can also determine the frequency. If your local market media plan calls for 300 GRPs in radio to support a two-week promotion, it would build an approximate 50 reach and an average frequency of 6 (300/ 50 = 6). Or, if you determined a monthly magazine reach of 50 was required, then your GRPs would equal 125 and your frequency is 2.5 (125/50 = 2.5). Exhibit 14.2 provides an overall GRP summary for television, radio, and magazine. For more accurate GRP data specific to your market, check with the appropriate media representatives.

To arrive at a rough approximation of reach and frequency data for each medium (other than television and radio), you can compute your own GRP data for magazines, newspaper, outdoor, and direct mail. However, for more precise data, you should contact your specific media representative. For your rough calculations use the following formulas.

- *Magazine:* Use % coverage for reach (circulation/total market households or total readers/target persons); number of insertions for frequency.

- *Newspaper:* Use % coverage for reach (circulation/total market households or total readers/target persons); number of insertions for frequency.

- *Outdoor:* For a standard four-week showing, estimate 50 showing = 85 reach and 15 frequency; 100 showing = 88 reach and 29 frequency.

- *Direct Mail:* Use percent coverage for reach (number mailed/total market target households or target persons); number of mailings for frequency.

Once you have estimated reach and frequency for a single medium, you may want to combine media weights with another medium. Although not an exact method (but good enough for approximation), you can use the grid in Exhibit 14.2 to arrive at combined weight levels across media. For example, 300 GRPs of radio and 800 GRPs of magazines are planned (1,100 GRPs total); and yield reaches of 50 and 80, respectively. Then, using the grid, the planner can see that the combined reach is approximately 86 (86 is at the intersection of row 50 and column 80); therefore, average frequency for the combined

EXHIBIT 14.1 Relationship of Reach, Frequency, and GRPs

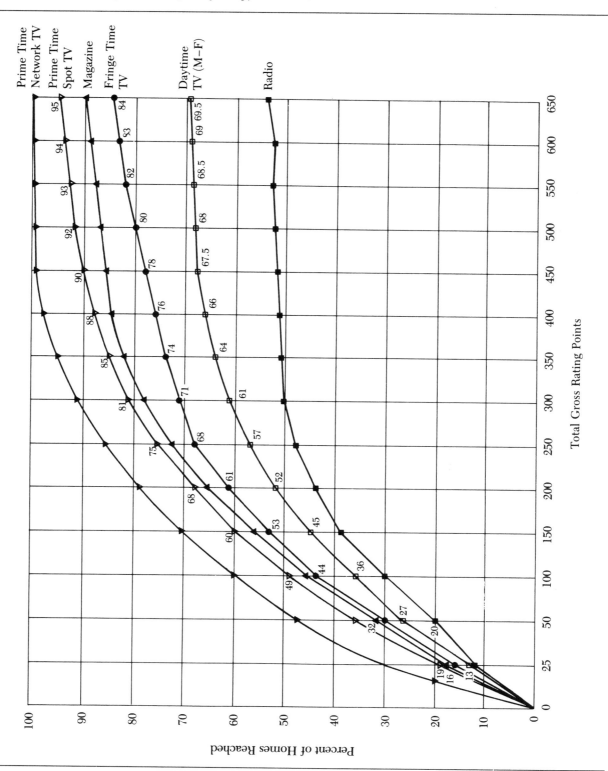

Source: Michael L. Rothschild, *Advertising, From Fundamentals to Strategies* (Lexington, Mass.: D.C. Health, 1987).

EXHIBIT 14.2   Accumulated Reach Levels Across Media

All Media Combinations (Homes and Individuals)

Reach

	5	10	15	20	25	30	35	40	45	50	55	60	65	70	75	80	85	90
5	10	14	19	24	28	33	38	43	47	52	57	62	66	71	76	81	85	90
10	14	19	23	27	32	36	40	45	50	54	59	63	68	72	77	81	86	91
15	19	23	27	31	35	39	43	48	52	56	61	65	69	73	78	82	86	91
20	24	27	31	35	38	42	46	50	55	59	63	67	71	75	79	83	87	91
25	28	32	35	38	41	44	48	53	57	61	64	68	72	76	79	83	87	92
30	33	36	39	42	44	47	51	55	59	63	66	70	73	77	80	84	88	92
35	38	40	43	46	48	51	53	58	62	65	68	71	75	78	81	84	88	92
40	43	45	48	50	53	55	58	60	64	67	70	73	76	79	82	85	88	92
45	47	50	52	55	57	59	62	64	66	69	72	75	77	80	83	86	89	93
50	52	54	56	59	61	63	65	67	69	71	74	76	79	81	84	86	89	93
55	57	59	61	63	64	66	68	70	72	74	76	78	80	82	85	87	90	93
60	62	63	65	67	68	70	71	73	75	76	78	80	82	84	86	88	90	94
65	66	68	69	71	72	73	75	76	77	79	80	82	83	85	86	88	91	94
70	71	72	73	75	76	77	78	79	80	81	82	84	85	86	87	89	91	94
75	76	77	78	79	79	80	81	82	83	84	85	86	86	87	88	89	91	95
80	81	81	82	83	83	84	84	85	86	86	87	88	88	89	89	90	92	95
85	85	86	86	87	87	88	88	88	89	89	90	90	91	91	91	92	92	95
90	90	91	91	91	92	92	92	92	93	93	93	94	94	94	95	95	95	95
95	95	95	96	96	96	96	96	96	97	97	97	97	97	97	98	98	98	98

Reach (left axis label)

Source: Michael L. Rothschild, *Advertising, From Fundamentals to Strategies* (Lexington, Mass.: D.C. Heath, 1987).

1,100 GRPs must be 12.8 (1,100/86 = 12.8). Although neither graph nor is perfectly accurate, each gives a good approximation for planning purposes.

How to Arrive at Quantitative Media Goals. Now that you understand media measurement, we can review different methods of arriving at communication weight level goals.

Macro Methods of Determining Media Weight Goal. Two macro, or market derived, methods can be used in determining the media weight goals for your product. One uses advertising as a percent of sales method based on industry averages, and the second uses a comparison of share of media to share of market sales. Both are market based; a third micro method is based on moving a specific target market to action. All three have their merits. You might apply a combination or decide to use one method that best fits.

The important point is that you understand how these different methods are employed to determine the media weight for your product.

The *advertising as a percent of sales method* begins with a review of the percent of sales allocated to advertising by the product category/industry in which you are competing. You could then use a similar percentage of your projected sales for your media budget after reducing this dollar budget by 10 to 15% to cover the cost of production to develop the ads or commercials:

Advertising percent of sales for category	3%
Product's projected sales	$1,000,000
Ad budget (3% x $1 million)	$30,000
Ad production of 10 percent (10% of $30,000 ad budget)	3,000
Available media budget ($30,000 – $3,000)	$27,000

Now that you have a dollar budget as a basis, you must next use this budget to determine a media weight goal. To arrive at a rough GRP weight level for your product, contact your media representative to arrive at a rough cost per rating point (CPP) by medium. For example,

Cost of average insertion or broadcast spot/Average rating = CPP

Or,

Average radio :60 commercial spot cost of $36/Average rating of 2 = $18 CPP

You can then divide the total media budget by the CPP for each medium to arrive at an approximate idea of how much media weight you can afford by each potential medium. For example,

$27,000/$18 CPP = 1,500 GRPs.

Although the above example is for a consumer medium, you could use a similar approach for business-to-business media using an average cost per point for each medium, such as trade publications and direct mail.

The advertising as percent of sales media weight goal approach is not very sophisticated, but it does challenge you to maximize the dollars in your media budget. However, keep in mind that because this approach is so broad in application, it does not take into consideration your current marketing situation or the competitive marketing environment. Therefore, advertising as a percent of sales should, in most situations, be a starting point and is only one method of arriving at the optimum media weight goal.

Another method of determining your media weight goal is the share comparison of media activity to sales—the *share of media voice versus share of market method*. This method compares your product's share of media voice (SOV) (in GRP media weight or media dollar expenditures as a percentage of total media advertising in your category or marketplace) to your product's share of market sales (SOM).

	SOV		SOM	
Organization	**$M**	**Percent**	**$MM**	**Percent**
A	$370	48%	$ 94.1	39.1%
B	230	29	70.0	29.1
C	69	9	38.6	16.1
D	105	14	38.0	15.7
Total	$774	100%	$240.7	100.0%

If you are using media dollar expenditures, take the media spending for each competitor, including your own product, from the business review and compare it to the corresponding shares of market. Is your share of media spending above or below that of the competition? Is your share of media spending above or below that of your product's share of market? Based on the direction of your marketing strategies and this SOV to SOM comparison, you can determine media weight goals.

As a very rough guide and only a starting point in using the SOV to SOM media weight determination, consider the following:

- Share of voice should approximate share of market.

- Usually, the greater the share of market, the greater the share of voice.

- If you want to increase your share of market, you most often should increase share of voice.

- If your share of voice is below your share of market year after year, your sales share will eventually decrease if everything in the competitive market environment and your marketing mix remains constant.

In using this method, keep in mind there is no guarantee that there always will be a direct cause and effect between an increase/decrease of SOV to match a similar increase/decrease in SOM. However, while there is not always perfect correlation, there is a directional cause and effect relationship between SOV and SOM.

Micro Target Market Method. Having reviewed media weight levels from a more marketwide or macro standpoint, it is also helpful to approach the setting of media weight goals on a specific target market or micro basis. With this approach, you attempt to determine what percentage of the target market must be reached and how often. You want to reach this target with the frequency necessary to build product awareness and understanding that will lead to a positive attitude toward the product and eventual purchase. In essence, you are attempting to determine the amount of GRP media weight necessary to effectively reach or communicate with a large enough portion of your target market to understand your message for the required sales.

A good place to start in determining the desired reach and frequency is to review your advertising objectives in terms of the percentage of target market you projected must have unaided awareness of your product and a predisposed attitude toward your product. Further, based on your marketing objectives, review what percentage of the target market you have estimated will try your product, make repeat purchases, and become regular users in order to meet the sales objectives.

It is also wise to review the media weight levels supporting your product over the past year (or better yet, three years), along with the level of media support for any promotions that may have been run. Based on these past supporting media weight levels, attempt to correlate sales results to determine what reach, frequency, and GRP levels are needed for this year's plan to help meet the estimated advertising and promotion objectives.

Depending on the type of product you are selling and its awareness and acceptance by the target market, every situation is different when setting reach goals. But as a suggested starting point, based on the authors' experience, you should consider a 60 to 90 or more reach of the target market. For a meaningful impact, it is usually necessary to reach well over one-half of the target market with your message. This is sometimes difficult to accomplish, particularly with short-term promotions and when the appropriate media vehicles are not readily available.

Once you have estimated your specific reach goals for the year, new product introduction, promotion, event, grand opening, etc., you must now estimate the frequency needed against the target to be reached in order to generate the effective reach necessary to elicit a specific response. In setting frequency goals, the required frequency to move the desired portion of the target market from product recognition to purchase is really a guesstimate. However, a potential range of frequency to make this happen is from a three to ten frequency. To determine whether you need more or less frequency depends on the following:

More Frequency	**Less Frequency**
New product	Established product
New campaign	Established campaign
Complex message	Simple message
Nonuser prospects (trial objective)	User prospects (repeat objective)
High competitive advertising levels	Low competitive advertising levels
Nonloyal user category, especially with short purchase cycle	Stable/loyal user base
Promotion/sales event	

It has been the experience of the authors, specifically with retail clients, that it is usually more successful to reach a smaller percentage of the target market with greater frequency than reach a larger percentage of the target market with minimum frequency. The reason is that it is better to have a smaller audience understand and remember your message than to reach a large audience but not have them thoroughly understand or remember the message.

To set a media weight goal, simply multiply your estimated reach by the total needed frequency for your total GRP level. For example:

$$\text{Reach 80} \times \text{Frequency 9} = \text{720 GRPs}$$

Keep in mind that with this methodology, the frequency of message exposure is based on average frequency. Some people within the target

EXHIBIT 14.3   Media Weight Guidelines

Product/Service Type	Target Audience GRP Weight Levels		
	Minimum Weekly	Seasonal/Event 4 Week Period	Annual
Consumer			
Package goods			
Established	75–150	300–600	1,000–3,000
Introductory/Promotional	150–250	600–1,000	1,800–5,000
Retail/Service			
Established	100–200	400–800	2,000–5,000
Introductory/Promotional	175–350	700–1,400	3,000–10,000
Business-to-Business			
Established	25–50	100–200	600–1,600
Introductory/Promotional	50–150	200–600	1,200–3,600

market will be exposed once and others at multiples of the average frequency number.

You probably have surmised from this discussion of setting media weight goals that there is no one hard and fast rule in determining the optimum media weight level for your product, but rather a composite of many factors to consider. However, to give you a starting point in setting your media weight goals, Exhibit 14.3 presents some guidelines for you to consider and we hope modify (possibly very dramatically) as you determine the media weight goals for your product. These *very rough* media weight guidelines are based on some quantitative data but primarily on the personal experience of the authors. Therefore they are subjective and must be used with extreme caution.

In the package goods area, the 2,500 to 5,000 annual introductory GRP level on the average can generate aided brand awareness of 60 to 80 percent and trial rates of up to 20 percent. In the retail environment, the 5,000 to 10,000 GRP level on the average can generate an unaided store awareness of 20 to 40 percent and trial rates of up to 20 percent. The trial rate in the retail environment is very dependent on store penetration (or the number of stores you have in the market).

Some examples of media weight goals for a nationally marketed package goods manufacturer would be:

To provide a minimum of 2,000 GRPs on a national basis for the fiscal year, or

To provide a reach of 90 to 95 and a minimum of average frequency of four over major media flight periods.

For a business-to-business manufacturer, an example of a media weight goal would be:

To reach a minimum of 80 percent of the target market a minimum of eight times annually.

Optional Media Budget Objective for Your Plan

Ideally, it usually is best to use the task method in building a media plan and thereby arrive at a media budget that is the direct result of the type and amount of media necessary to fulfill the communication goals. This type of media budget is then further refined, based on the cumulative marketing plan budget considerations, to implement all the elements of the market mix. However, if there are specific financial media parameters for the media plan, many times they are included as part of the media objectives. Some examples of media budget objectives would be to maintain total media expenditures at 3-1/2 percent of total projected sales, or to execute an annual media plan at the $300,000 budget level.

Step 3: Prepare the Media Strategy

Under media strategy you should include the following:

- *A brief summary of the media mix.* This describes the different media to be used—magazines, direct mail, radio, etc.

- *The specific use of each medium.* This is a tactical description of how each of the specific media is to be used, such as magazine types, ad size, broadcast programming/daypart type, and length of commercials.

- *The scheduling of the media.* A decription in terms of when each medium is used and at what levels.

Media Mix Strategy

Value Comparison. Before you write a media mix strategy, you must first review and evaluate which media will best fulfill the media objectives. To begin your evaluation, do a quick initial screen of the different media (newspaper, radio, etc.), determining which have a possibility of use in a media plan that will meet the objectives. It is a good idea to do this quick screen of *all* media to ensure that you do not automatically rule out a medium based on your preconceived notions or without determining whether it could meet the objectives. (See Exhibit 14.4) If you do not understand the strengths and weaknesses of each medium, you can review an advertising or media text or check with the appropriate media representatives.

Arriving at the Right Media Mix. To arrive at the appropriate mix of media, you must screen out the obviously inappropriate media; do a quantitative and qualitative analysis of the potential media candidates; consider how your media selection will impact on the target market in relationship to the competitive media environment.

Screen Out Inappropriate Media. After reviewing the strengths and weaknesses of each medium in terms of its appropriateness for meeting the media objectives, screen out those media that logically could not meet the objectives. If you are marketing a new product to a broad general market that requires emotional image advertising, you would not use direct mail; if the product was very technical and required detailed explanation, you would not use outdoor; if you were grand opening a 1,000 square foot ice cream shop in a suburb of Chicago, you would not use television.

EXHIBIT 14.4 Communication Values by Medium

Television

Pros: Audiovisual impact, most intrusive, demands less active involvement relative to print, immediate impact, quick reach and good frequency, relatively homogenous national coverage, broad homogenous local coverage that goes beyond metro areas.

Cons: Limited to commercial length constraints, one exposure per expenditure.

Radio

Pros: Good frequency medium, demands less active involvement, good localized spot coverage for city/metro area.

Cons: Audio impact only, low ratings, limited to commercial length time constraints, one exposure per expenditure, reach builds slower than television or newspaper.

Local Newspaper

Pros: Immediate impact, high reach potential, coupons get redeemed more quickly, very timely.

Cons: Low readers per copy, very little pass along, very short life span, limited in production quality.

Sunday Supplements

Pros: Immediate impact, high reach potential, good coupon carrier, better production quality than newspaper.

Cons: Low readers per copy, very little pass along, very short life span, not as flexible in timing as newspaper.

Consumer Magazines

Pros: No time constraints per message, potential for multiple exposures per expenditure, in-depth product description potential, generally upscale demography, pass along readership, coupon/promotion delivery vehicle, good production quality.

Cons: Visual impact only, requires active involvement, less immediate impact, lower reach and local market coverage than television, radio, or newspaper.

Business-to-Business/Trade Publications

Pros: In-depth product description potential, reaches relatively small but targeted audience, ads and editorial area highly read, coupon carrier, low cost per inquiry.

Cons: Visual impact only.

Outdoor/Out of Home

Pros: Good for product/package identification, good reach, high frequency, good directional vehicle, local geographic concentration.

Cons: Visual impact only, limited copy development potential, very high total monthly cost for anything approaching national coverage.

Direct Mail

Pros: Extensive copy development potential, very selective, easy to track response, excellent coupon carrier, flexible in terms of timing and types of inclusions per mailing.

Cons: Visual impact only, easy to discard.

Evaluate Each Medium on a CPM Quantitative Basis. After eliminating those media that will obviously not meet the objectives, compare the remaining media on a quantitative cost per thousand (CPM) basis to determine media efficiency. A CPM is used as a common denominator for media comparison.

To arrive at a CPM for a medium, you can either divide target audience into the medium cost multiplied by 1,000 (Cost/Audience x 1,000 = CPM) or move the decimal point of the audience three places to the left and divide into the medium cost (Cost/Audience/1,000 = CPM). If a network prime time television :30 commercial cost is $88,245, and the number of target persons reached is 10,415,000, then $88,245/10,415 = $8.47 CPM. You will want to evaluate on a CPM basis each of the potential media in your marketplace that you have screened and deemed appropriate for your product. To more easily compare medium CPMs, you might want to rank order each medium from the lowest to highest CPM. Having reviewed the ranked media CPMs, you can begin to eliminate those media with high CPMs. However, you cannot automatically assume that those with the lowest CPM should be included in your media mix. You must also consider the most appropriate medium for each product and the competition's use of the media. In the final analysis, it is not always the lowest CPM but the lowest cost per sale (CPS). What may appear to be too costly based on a pure CPM evaluation might be the most effective medium in terms of selling goods.

Competitive Media Mix Considerations. You must consider the competition's use of the media mix. What is their media mix selection? When do they use each medium? At what levels? How do they use each medium in relation to the others? If a competitor with a considerably larger media budget dominates the medium that would have been your first choice, you might decide to concentrate all your media dollars in your second choice, where you can dominate and where you will not have your media effort diluted.

The point should be made here that with or without competition, it is usually better to concentrate your media dollars in a few media to achieve continuous reach and high frequency than to dilute your media dollars over many different media, thereby fragmenting your media effort. However, the more competition you have in the media, the more it becomes necessary for you to do a good job in one medium before placing weight in another. Make sure that each additional medium added to the media mix is used with weight levels that will have competitive impact and generate effective reach.

Media Mix Strategy Examples. After you have evaluated the media alternatives from quantitative, appropriateness, and competitive points of view, you must write your media mix strategy. The following are examples for a national package goods client and a business-to-business crafts manufacturer, respectively:

> Use a combination of network television for national coverage and spot television in the designated high opportunity markets of Chicago, Los Angeles, and Philadelphia.

> Use national trade publications across a minimum of two top craft magazines to broaden reach potential of both primary and secondary target audiences.

Specific Usage of Each Medium

Within this media strategy section, define the specific tactical usage of each medium to be employed, based again on the media objectives. Include the following medium specifics where they apply.

- *Television and Radio*—Daypart TV: Day, Fringe, Prime Time, News, Sports. Daypart radio: AM Drive, Mid-Day, PM Drive, Night. Program types. Length of commercial.

- *Magazine*—Type (news weeklies, sports, etc.). Specific magazines by name. Ad size. Position. Black and white; one-, two-, three-, or four-color.

- *Newspaper*—Daily, weekly, and shopper (nonpaid). Ad size. Section of paper. Black and white; one-, two-, three-, and four-color. Day of week.

- *Outdoor*—Level of showing (25/50/100). Special location or directional requirements. Size if not 30 sheet. Other specifics: painted, rotary, etc.

- *Direct Mail*—Size (height/width). Number of pages. Quantity. Black and white/color specifics.

Medium Usage Strategy Examples. Some examples of media vehicle strategy/tactic statements for a package goods food client would be as follows:

Use full-page, four-color ads in women's service magazines—*Women's Day, Family Circle, Ladies Home Journal,* and *Good Housekeeping*—and general interest magazines—*People* and *TV Guide.*

For a regional retailer, some examples would be as follows:

Use a :30 television daypart mix of 30 percent daytime, 30 percent general fringe, 20 percent prime time, and 20 percent late news.

Use 1/3-page newspaper ads for continuity and 1/2-page to full-page ads to support major promotions on Thursdays in the main news section.

Scheduling Strategy

Along with the selection of the optimum medium, media vehicle, and ad size/commercial length, you must also determine how the media should run. While the seasonality media objective provides guidelines for when to advertise throughout the year, the scheduling strategy provides specific direction of how the media is to be run.

Scheduling Approaches. There are a number of different strategic approaches to scheduling.

- *Continuity schedules* are, continuous and run at a relatively fixed, even level to help sustain nonseasonal/nonpromotional sales.

- *Heavy-up schedules* incorporate incremental media weight to support periods of higher market activity, new product or campaign introductions, grand openings, and promotions.

- *Pulsing schedules* run in a continuous on/off pattern, such as the media runs two weeks, then is off two weeks, on two weeks, off two weeks, etc. The on/off pattern is repeated on a regular basis. The pulsing schedule provides more media support when advertising, which helps cut through the media noise level in the market, making the advertising stand out from that of the competition.

- *Flighting in scheduling* is generally three to six weeks of continuous advertising followed by hiatus periods or periods of no advertising. Flighting is used for short-term promotions and events, product introductions, and during periods of high seasonal sales.

- *Front loading* is the running of heavier weight levels with the commencement of a media schedule when you kick off seasonal advertising, new advertising campaigns, new product introductions/grand openings, promotions, and trade show announcements.

Scheduling Strategy Examples. Some examples of scheduling strategies for a package goods product are:

To schedule a higher level of prime time television during the new creative introductory period, or

To maintain strong levels of daytime television throughout all flights.

For business-to-business advertisers, some scheduling strategies are:

To schedule continuity magazine advertising to run alternating months, or

To schedule direct mail drops in months when magazine ads do not run.

Step 4: Develop the Final Media Plan with Calendar and Budget

Prepare and Review Alternative Media Plans

Having already set media objectives and strategies, you should by now have solidified your media thinking. You are now ready to rough out in calendar form a graphic representation of at least two potential media plans. Exhibit 14.5 presents a calendar for a hospital media plan. A blank planning calendar is provided at the end of this chapter. You should prepare alternative plans in terms of different media included, usage of each medium, scheduling, total media weight levels, and budgets. Then compare the alternative plans in terms of total weight placed against the target market (reach, frequency, and GRPs). Also, compare corresponding costs to determine which plan meets the media objectives, maximizing the delivery of the message to the target audience at the lowest cost.

Prepare a Media Budget Summary

Along with a finalized media flow chart calendar, also include a media budget that you can exhibit in a number of different ways depending on the needs of your marketing plan. Two media budget work charts are included at the end of this chapter. The first details spending for each medium by quarter. If you want to present more spending detail, you can break out your dollars for each medium by month using a similar budget format. If you want to show both weight levels and spending, you can detail GRPs/TRPs and dollars for each quarter or month using a similar format.

If you have included a number of different products or markets in the marketing plan that require specific media support, you should use the second budget work chart provided that details media spending by product/market and medium. It is best to show your media budget summary in the media section and then include media totals as part of the total marketing plan budget, which is included at the end of the marketing plan document (discussed in Chapter 17).

EXHIBIT 14.5   Media Calendar for Hospital Advertising Campaign

1993 Media Calendar

Monday (Bdcst) Dates

General Hospital
Madison DMA
October 7, 1992

Media	Advertising Program	JAN–DEC schedule	Total Target Rating Points (TRP's)
Adults 25-54	SUSTAINING / NEW SERVICE INTRODUCTION / EMERGENCY AND OBSTETRICS / SUSTAINING		
Television :30's Madison DMA	300 TRP'S PER WEEK / 200/WEEK		5300
20% Day, 50% Fringe, 30% Prime	200 TRP'S PER WEEK		
13 Weeks at 200 TRP's/Per Week			
9 Weeks at 300 TRP's Per Week			
Radio :60's Madison Metro	200 TRP'S/WEEK		1200
1/3 AM, 1/3 Day, 1/3 PM			
6 Weeks at 200 TRP's/Per Week			
4 Stations			
20 Spots Per Station Per Week			
Newspaper - Journal and Times	1 INSERTION PER WEEK		554
1/4 Page Weekday (B/W)			
8 Insertions			
Newspaper - Journal and Times	1 INSERTION PER WEEK		346
1/2 Page Sunday (B/W)			
5 Insertions			
Outdoor: #100 Showing	600–625 TRP'S/PER WEEK / 600–625 TRP'S PER WEEK		15312
25 Locations Per 100 Showing			

Total Rating Points: 22712

Week-ending dates across top: JAN 28 4 11 18 25 | FEB 1 8 15 22 | MAR 1 8 15 22 29 | APR 5 12 19 26 | MAY 3 10 17 24 31 | JUN 7 14 21 28 | JUL 5 12 19 26 | AUG 2 9 16 23 | SEP 30 6 13 20 27 | OCT 4 11 18 25 | NOV 1 8 15 22 29 | DEC 6 13 20

Worksheet 14.1   Media Plan

Media Objectives

Target Audience

Geography

Seasonality

Media Weight Goals

Budget (Optional)

Rationale for Objectives

Worksheet 14.1   Media Plan (Continued)

Media Strategies

Media Mix

Specific Medium Usage

Scheduling

Rationale for Strategies

Worksheet 14.2

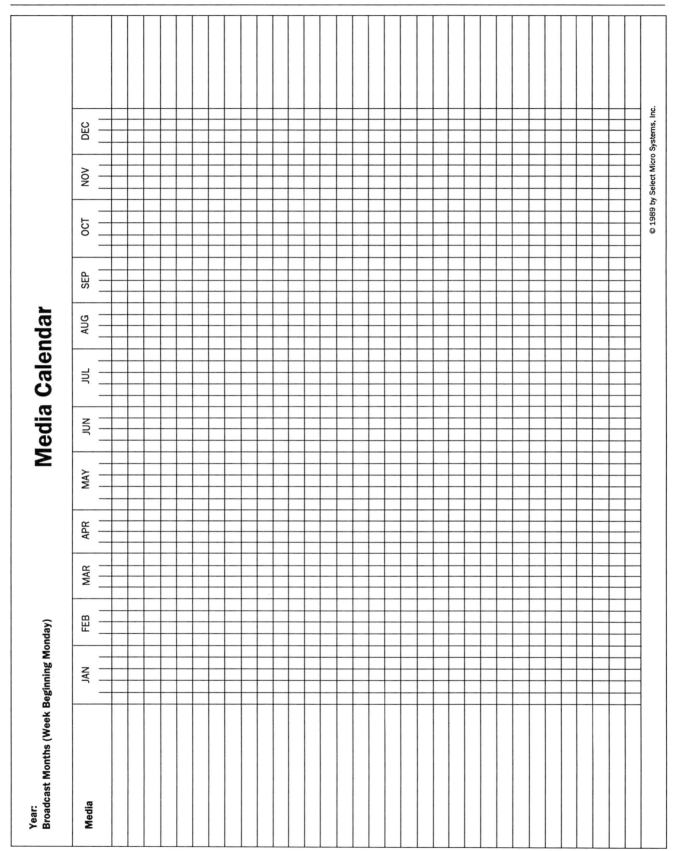

Media Calendar

Year:
Broadcast Months (Week Beginning Monday)

Media

JAN | FEB | MAR | APR | MAY | JUN | JUL | AUG | SEP | OCT | NOV | DEC

© 1989 by Select Micro Systems, Inc.

Worksheet 14.3   Media Budget

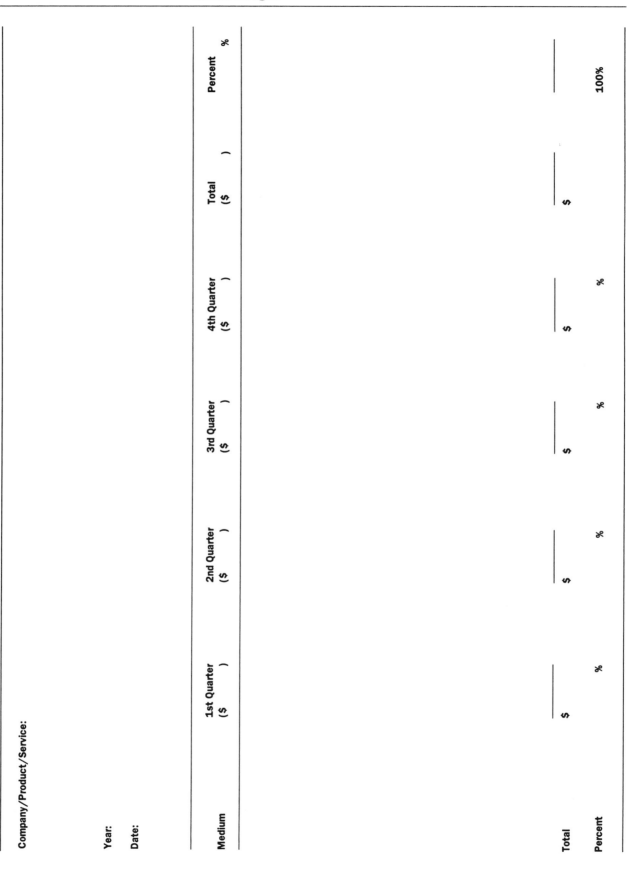

Spending by Medium and Quarter

Company/Product/Service:

Year:

Date:

Medium	1st Quarter ($)	2nd Quarter ($)	3rd Quarter ($)	4th Quarter ($)	Total ($)	Percent %
Total	$	$	$	$	$	
Percent	%	%	%	%		100%

Spending by Product/Market and Medium

Company/Product/Service:

Year:

Date:

Medium Product/Market	$( ) Percent	$( ) Percent	$( ) Percent	$( ) Percent	$( ) Percent	$( ) Percent	Total Spending by Product/Market ($) Percent

| Total Spending by Medium | $ ____ % | $ ____ % | $ ____ % | $ ____ % | $ ____ % | $ ____ % | $ ____ 100% |

Merchandising

Now that you have developed promotion and advertising plans and decided how to deliver their message through your media plan, it is time to focus on how non-media communication can enhance the effectiveness of your overall marketing program.

DEFINITION

We define merchandising as the method to communicate product information and promotions through *non-media communication vehicles*. Merchandising is a way to make non-media visual or written statements about your company with or without one-on-one personal communication. Merchandising includes brochures, sell sheets, product displays, video presentations, banners, posters, shelf talkers, table tents, or any other tools that can be used to communicate product attributes, positioning, pricing, or promotion information through non-media vehicles.

Merchandising communication can be delivered through the following methods:

- *Personal Sales Presentation:* Often brochures, sell sheets, and other forms of merchandising are used to enhance a personal sales visit. The material can guide the sales visit, provide visual and factual support of the sales presentation, and serve as a leave behind for the customer or prospect to reference.

- *Point-of-Purchase:* In many product categories, over two-thirds of the actual purchase decisions are actually made at the point of purchase. For this reason, merchandising is a useful tool at the point of purchase to influence in-store purchase decisions. Merchandising materials can also be utilized at the point of purchase in the form of shelf talkers, table tents in restaurants, product displays, banners, etc. Merchandising at the point of purchase allows the marketer to make an impact on the purchaser above and beyond what can be expected of a product's packaging.

- *Events:* Merchandising is implemented through special events or company functions where contact with the target market occurs through sales meetings, conventions, mass participation events, concerts, etc. Banners, product displays, or fliers are commonly used at mass participation events to communicate brand name and product benefits to consumers.

Geography, timing, and purpose are also part of merchandising. Your merchandising plan should address where your merchandising programs will be executed. Will they be national, regional, local, or even in selected stores within a market?

It is also necessary to determine the timing of the merchandising execution in relation to the other marketing mix elements. For example, your plan may require a brochure to be delivered prior to sales visits or after the advertising campaign kick off. Or you may want a retail store's featured inventory displayed for the duration of an advertising media blitz.

What is the purpose of merchandising? What is it to accomplish? You need to describe what marketing tool merchandising will be assisting. Will you be merchandising product attributes, a new or lower price, a promotion, an advertising message, a personal sell-in presentation, etc.? In summary, you must decide on the communication focus of the merchandising before writing this merchandising segment of the marketing plan.

HOW TO DEVELOP A MERCHANDISING PLAN

A worksheet for you to use in developing your merchandising objectives and strategies is provided at the end of this chapter.

Step 1: Establish Merchandising Objectives

Your merchandising objectives should include the following:

- The number of merchandising pieces delivered or displayed at specific target locations

- The geography

- The timing

- The communication focus

The following are some examples of merchandising objectives:

Achieve placement of the new product display, communicating the product's benefits, in 40 percent of the grocery stores carrying the product line nationwide in the month of September.

Obtain placement of price promotional tents June through August in 50 percent of the current accounts in the top ten markets.

Display four product banners at each event during the concert series in all markets.

Step 2: Establish Merchandising Strategies

Your merchandising strategies should detail how to achieve your objectives in the following areas:

- The delivery and display method to be used

- How to achieve placement of the merchandising elements

- Description of creative parameters for development of the merchandising materials

Examples of merchandising strategies include the following:

Use the personal sales force to deliver the brochure during sales presentations.

Obtain placement of the shelf talkers by offering a competitive discount on each case in return for participation in the shelf talker program.

Obtain placement of the brand identification banners by the sales force. Employ a weekly monitoring system to ensure that the banners remain in place for the four-week period.

The shelf talkers should incorporate visible brand identification and highlight the rules of the sweepstakes. An entry pad should be included.

Worksheet 15.1   Merchandising

Merchandising Objectives

Merchandising Strategies

Rationale

Publicity

This is the last marketing mix tool to include in your marketing plan. In most cases, publicity will play a key but less important role in your marketing plan than many of the other marketing tools.

DEFINITION

In this book, we will define publicity as *nonpaid media communication* that helps build target market awareness and positively affects attitudes for your product or firm. Publicity provides your firm or product with a benefit not found in any other marketing mix tool. Since publicity utilizes nonpaid communication through independent news media, it adds a dimension of legitimacy that can't be found in advertising. Obtaining publicity for your firm or product can be difficult, with no guarantees on placement or what is ultimately communicated, since publicity is nonpaid and to a large degree non-controllable.

Before incorporating a publicity segment in your marketing plan, you should ask yourself three questions:

- Do you need and want the added dimension of legitimacy in your overall communications effort?

- Do you need additional media weight without media dollar investment, knowing that there is no certainty of the amount (if any) and type of publicity you will receive?

- Are you willing to make the investment in time, through either your company staff or an outside agency, to garnish publicity knowing its upside and downside? Will this investment be worth it?

Also, keep in mind that publicity is only one part of public relations. Public relations is very encompassing and deals with creating goodwill for an organization and affecting long-term public opinion issues. If you need in-depth information on public relations, refer to a text exclusively devoted to this subject. Finally, keep in mind that publicity doesn't just happen. In most instances, positive publicity is the result of a written, well-thought-out plan and a hands-on executed program.

Included in the publicity section of the marketing plan should be target market, objectives, and strategies. In most cases there are two target markets—the media to be made aware of the news story, and the target market to whom

206

you want to communicate it. Before planning your annual publicity program, make sure you review the relevant problems, opportunities, and marketing strategies. In addition, make sure that you thoroughly understand the interests of your *product's* target market and those of the *media* target market. Further, make sure before you prepare your publicity plan that you have clearly delineated what you want to accomplish with this marketing tool.

HOW TO DEVELOP A PUBLICITY PLAN

A worksheet to use in developing your publicity objectives and strategies is provided at the end of this chapter..

Step 1: Establish Your Publicity Objectives

Your publicity objectives should be specific and measurable and relate to a specific time period similar to your marketing, advertising, and promotion objectives. However, since publicity is not a paid, controlled message, it does not usually focus on affecting a target market behavior but rather on making the target market aware of the product or company in a positive light. Your publicity objectives should address the following:

- The specific purpose of the publicity effort (e.g., announce a grand opening, gain additional exposure for a new product, generate support through a public service announcement (PSA), etc.)

- The specific target market (medium and audience)

- The time period and marketplace

- The expected level of exposure, by medium, to be generated from the publicity effort

An example of a publicity objective would be:

To achieve maximum exposure in the next year among sewers for the grand opening events through the television, radio, and newspaper media in each of the 20 DMA markets,

To obtain coverage from a minimum of two television stations and a minimum of three radio stations, or

To obtain coverage from a minimum of one news-paper before and after the event.

Step 2: Establish Your Publicity Strategies

Publicity strategies describe how to achieve the media coverage delineated in the publicity objectives. Address the following in formulating your strategies:

- Placement and type of news releases or stories

- Coverage via interviews and/or news conferences with television, radio, newspaper, and magazine editor representatives

- Participation in talk shows and local interest programs such as *PM Magazine*

- Visibility at conventions, seminars, and public events
- Public service announcements (if you are a nonprofit organization or can develop a joint effort with a nonprofit organization)
  In developing your publicity strategies, also consider the following:

- *Make sure the news media is thoroughly aware of the event or product's news.* For example, you may write news releases and deliver them in a memorable way.

- *Detail a specific follow-up procedure.* Make certain the news releases weren't forgotten or lost and, most importantly, will be used in some manner.

- *Develop ways to tie the media into the publicity event itself.* Or obtain a third party to help legitimize your requests for publicity support. For example, provide cosponsorship packages to media and charities in return for publicity. The media and charity cosponsors become cosponsors on all paid, printed advertising in return for predetermined publicity requirements both before and during the event.

- *Provide a unique twist to interest the media.* This can be communicated in a news release or by phone to the media to pique their interest. Or provide a chance for an exclusive interview in return for media coverage. This technique worked very well for our Famous Footwear client. Major news media were offered the chance to interview all-pro football player Al Toon of the New York Jets in return for publicity surrounding the opening of a new Famous Footwear store.

- *Where possible, include memorable, appropriate product identification.*

The following are examples of publicity strategies that could be developed to achieve a hypothetical publicity objective. Assume you are developing publicity strategies for the following publicity objective: "Achieve maximum radio and newspaper exposure in each market among young adults age 18 to 24 for the five concerts to be staged in the next year, in five DMA markets to be determined."

At a minimum, get coverage from two of the top five young adult radio stations.

At a minimum, get coverage from a major daily before and after the event.

Potential publicity strategies would be as follows:

Prepare four different news releases, each with a different newsworthy slant on the event to be delivered via mail and personally before and after the event.

Stress the various benefits to the charity in the news release, particularly how important the event is in regard to the charity's yearly fundraising.

Have the local press interview the concert performers and the local charity spokesperson incorporating company identification at the interview site.

Worksheet 16.1   Publicity

Objectives

Strategies

Rationale

STEP EIGHT

Marketing Plan Budget and Calendar

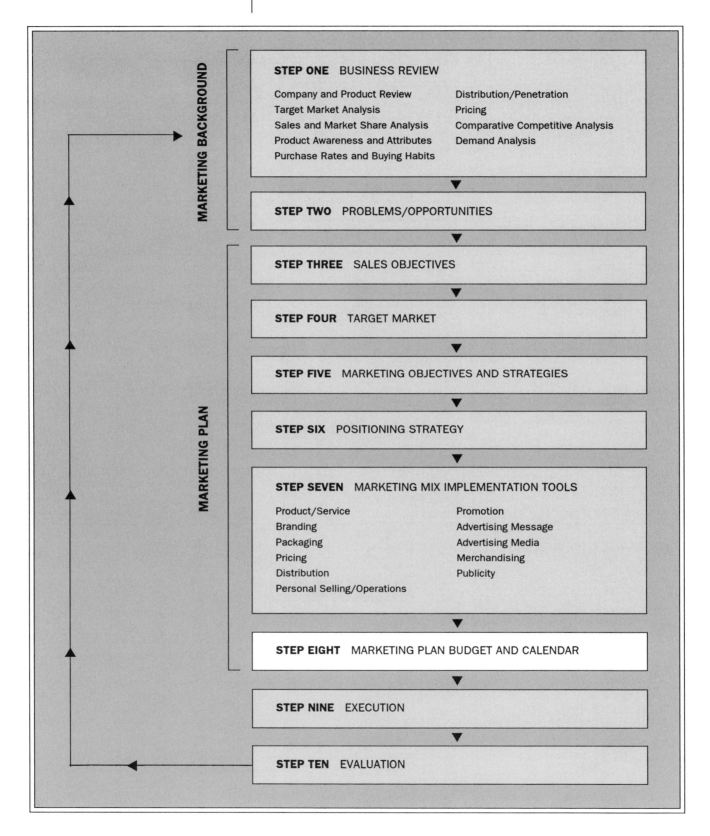

MARKETING BACKGROUND

STEP ONE BUSINESS REVIEW

Company and Product Review
Target Market Analysis
Sales and Market Share Analysis
Product Awareness and Attributes
Purchase Rates and Buying Habits

Distribution/Penetration
Pricing
Comparative Competitive Analysis
Demand Analysis

STEP TWO PROBLEMS/OPPORTUNITIES

MARKETING PLAN

STEP THREE SALES OBJECTIVES

STEP FOUR TARGET MARKET

STEP FIVE MARKETING OBJECTIVES AND STRATEGIES

STEP SIX POSITIONING STRATEGY

STEP SEVEN MARKETING MIX IMPLEMENTATION TOOLS

Product/Service
Branding
Packaging
Pricing
Distribution
Personal Selling/Operations

Promotion
Advertising Message
Advertising Media
Merchandising
Publicity

STEP EIGHT MARKETING PLAN BUDGET AND CALENDAR

STEP NINE EXECUTION

STEP TEN EVALUATION

Marketing Budget, Payback Analysis, and Marketing Calendar

Now that you have completed the objectives and strategies for each tool of your marketing plan, you need to prepare a budget, project a payback from the results of your marketing effort, and develop a marketing calendar. This process involves three separate steps.

- Develop a budget to provide estimated costs associated with each marketing tool used in the marketing plan.

- Utilize a payback analysis to determine whether the results of your marketing plan will produce adequate revenues to meet sales and profit goals. If the payback indicates that your plan will not allow you to meet sales and profit goals, you may need to revise your budget or your marketing plan objectives and subsequent strategies and executions.

- Once you have reconciled your budget and payback analysis, a marketing calendar should be developed to provide a summary of all marketing executions in one visual presentation.

BUDGETING OVERVIEW

Based on our experience, no matter what budgeting approach is employed, it seems there are never enough marketing dollars. For this reason, the marketer needs to determine priorities for the plan, along with corresponding executional costs for the various marketing activities. Then, based on the priorities and associated costs, pare back the activities to meet the predetermined budget level, striking a balance between what must be accomplished and what you can realistically afford. Ideally, you will be able to develop a budget that is realistic from a total spending standpoint and yet will provide the necessary resources to support a successful marketing plan.

HOW TO DEVELOP YOUR BUDGET

Step 1: Percent of Sales

The first step in developing a budget for your marketing plan is to review the amount spent on advertising/media, promotion, and total marketing by other firms in your industry. Usually, an industry standard exists that will provide the average percent of sales that will account for the advertising/media budget, the promotion budget, and sometimes even the total marketing budget.

The major disadvantage with this method is that it creates a situation where sales determine marketing expenditures. However, the whole idea behind disciplined campaign development is the belief that marketing affects sales. With the percent of sales method, when sales decline and there are problems to be solved, there is less money available to solve them.

The method makes most sense if used as a way to determine a starting point. This is how we recommend you use this method—as a first step in developing your budget. Additionally, if your firm has no real history with the effects of marketing and advertising, then the percent of sales method will act as a way to allocate expenditures that should be fairly consistent with industry standards. You can find the industry advertising to sales ratios for the Standard Industrial Classification (SIC) codes in a published report by Schonfeld and Associates. *Advertising Age* also publishes the advertising to sales ratios of the top 100 advertisers each year. Another source is *Fairchild Fact Files,* a publication that provides information on individual consumer industries. Annual reports and 10-Ks are another excellent source for this information.

Step 2: Task Method

The second step in developing a budget is to utilize the task method. This method attempts to develop a budget that will adequately support the marketing mix activity in your plan to achieve the sales and marketing objectives. To arrive at the total dollar budget, you must estimate the costs for each marketing tool execution involved in the plan. The assumption is that through a disciplined planning process, challenging yet realistic sales objectives were established, along with a marketing plan to meet those objectives. Thus, the budget will allow the objectives to be met efficiently. An aggressive marketing plan will result in a more aggressive budget utilizing this method. However there is no real test of affordability or profitability, which is why a payout analysis is presented in the payout section of this chapter.

Step 3: Competitive Method

The final step for consideration is to attempt estimating the sales and marketing budgets of the leading competitive firms. Then compare these estimates to your sales and marketing budget. This method might allow your firm to match or beat specific competitive expenditures, helping to assure that you remain competitive in the marketplace. The advantage of this method is that it provides the potential for an immediate response to competitive actions. The disadvantages are that it is difficult to estimate competitors' budgets and it does not consider the inherent potential of your firm based on data developed from the business review. Utilizing this method alone, you may be restricting the actual potential of your firm based on your competitors' lack of insight and marketing ability.

FINALIZING SUPPORT

If the data are available, we recommend using a combination of all three steps in finalizing your marketing budget. First use the percent of sales method to provide a guideline budget figure based on your product's historical spending and that of the marketplace. Used properly, the percent of sales number will help provide insight into whether you might be starting too low or too high based on the experiences of other similar companies in your industry.

Next, use the task method. This will provide you with a budget that will be your best chance to achieve the stated objectives in your own marketing plan. The task method is not as biased nor is it limiting in that the budget is derived based solely on what is required to provide for the success of your individual marketing plan. Product history and industry averages play a lesser role in this budgeting process. However, if the task method budget varies substantially from the percent of sales method budget, you need to review the reasons why your plan requires either substantially more or less expenditures than the industry average. If, for example, you are introducing a new product, you may be required to spend at greater levels than the industry average to obtain initial trial of the new product while still maintaining sales of your existing lines.

Finally, consider using the competitive budgeting method as a device to help you respond to competitive pressures in the marketplace. If your company is consistently spending less than a major competitor, and you are losing market share while this competitor is gaining market share, then perhaps you might develop a budget that allows you to be more competitive from a spending standpoint. There is not much any marketer can do, no matter how sophisticated, if continually and dramatically outspent by the competition.

HOW TO DEVELOP YOUR BUDGET FORMAT

In preparing your budget, you should begin with a rationale that outlines what the budget is designed to accomplish. The rationale covers:

- Restatement of the sales goals

- Marketing objectives

- Geography parameters

- Plan time frame

Following the rationale is a breakout of planned expenses by line item under each expense category. The budget line item categories include all applicable marketing mix tools along with any other miscellaneous marketing expense items such as research. The example shown in Exhibit 17.1 can serve as a prototype for your budgeting process. The only difference between this budget and one you may develop is that your budget may have more line item expense categories. (A worksheet is provided at the end of this chapter.) If you will be developing new products, there will be a new product development expense category. If you include publicity in your plan, this marketing tool will also have a budget line item.

EXHIBIT 17.1   Heartland 1993 Marketing Plan Budget

Rationale

The budget for the fiscal year is designed to:

1. Provide support necessary to meet the aggressive sales goal of increasing store for store sales 15 percent over the previous year.
2. Provide support necessary to meet the systemwide marketing objectives of:

Increase existing customer purchasing rates from 1.2 to 2 purchases per year.

Initiate new trial, increasing the customer base 20 percent above current levels of 5,000 active customers per store.

Marketing Mix Tool (Nov. 5, 1993)	$M	Percent of Total Budget
Media		
Television (6 markets)	$350.0	31.8%
900 TRP's :30's		
900 TRP's :10's		
Newspaper (12 markets)	202.0	18.3
30, 1/3 page insertions		
Direct mail (12 markets/24 stores)	120.0	10.9
10,000 per store per drop		
Postage (4 drops per year)		
Media total	$672.0	61.0%
Production		
Television	$100.0	9.1
2 :30 and 3 :10 spots (to be used for two years)		
Newspaper	18.0	1.6
Type, photography/illustration for 30 ads		
Direct mail (12 markets/24 stores)	100.0	9.1
Four direct mail drops, 240M pieces per drop		
Photography, type, printing		
Production total	$218.0	19.8%
Promotion		
Redemption cost	$120.0	10.9
Redemption cost of $5 off coupon in two of the four mailings		
Estimated response of 5 percent		
5 percent x 480,000 mailing = 24,000		
24,000 x $5 = $120,000		
Media		
Media costs calculated in media section		
Production		
Product costs calculated in production section		
Promotion total	$120.0	10.9%
Merchandising		
Store signage	$30.0	2.7
20 signs per store per month to support planned media promotions and in-store promotions		
Point-of-purchase displays	10.0	0.9
Two p-o-p displays per store to support the April and December promotions		
Merchandising total	$40.0	3.6%
Selling Costs		
Sales incentive programs	$20.0	1.8
Sales total	$20.0	1.8%

EXHIBIT 17.1   Heartland 1993 Marketing Plan Budget (Continued)

Marketing Mix Tool (Nov. 5, 1990)		$M	Percent of Total Budget
Research Costs			
Market research		$32.0	2.9
Marketwide	$20.0		
In-store	$12.0		
Research total		$32.0	2.9%
Total budget estimate		$1,102.0	100.0%
Total sales estimate		$24,000.0	
Marketing budget as a percent of sales		4.6 percent	
Total Budget Compared to Industry Average and Previous Year			
Marketing as a percent of sales per plan:		1,102	4.6
Marketing as a percent of sales per industry average:			4.0
Index company budget to industry average: 115*			
Index company budget to previous year ($1,000M/$1,102M): 110			
Total Planned Budget Compared to Competition†			
Total planned budget for Company:		1,102	4.6
Total estimated budget Competitor A:		2,000	4.5
Total estimated budget Competitor B:		1,000	5.5

*In this example the planned budget would be 15 points above the industry average for marketing as a percent of sales and 10 points above the previous year's plan.

†If the data exists, we recommend that this analysis be accomplished on an individual market basis and a national basis. This will help demonstrate localized geographic spending policies of competitors.

PAYBACK ANALYSIS OVERVIEW

An important part of any budget is the payback analysis. The payback analysis provides the marketer with a projection of whether the marketing plan or specific marketing programs in the plan will generate revenues in excess of expenses. The payback analysis should review both short-run and long-run projected sales and associated costs to estimate the initial program payback in year one and the projected payback in the second and third year.

Reconciling Your Budget and Payback Analysis

If the payback analysis shows that the marketing plan dollar investment cannot be justified, a rethinking and adjustment of sales objectives and marketing plan objectives, strategies, use of the marketing mix tools, and budget expenditures is needed. After this is accomplished, another payback analysis is needed to further determine if the new plan will meet payback expectations.

How to Develop Your Payback Analysis

We recommend using one of two payback methodologies: the contribution to fixed costs or the gross margin to net sales.

Contribution to Fixed Overhead Payback Analysis

Many retailers, service organizations, and sometimes manufacturers use a contribution to fixed costs payback. It focuses on two sets of figures: (1) sales and revenues, and (2) all direct marketing costs associated with the sale of the product to the consumer.

Contribution to fixed costs, or overhead payback results, are determined by first calculating estimated gross sales and then subtracting cost of goods sold to derive a gross profit on sales figure. Next all variable selling expenses directly associated with the sales of the product (selling costs, advertising and media expenditures, etc.) are subtracted from the gross profit figure to provide a contribution to fixed costs figure. This method can be utilized to analyze individual marketing programs or a whole year's plan.

The contribution to fixed costs method is utilized because it accurately demonstrates the results of the marketing executions. Only the revenues and expenses directly attributed to each marketing effort are utilized in the analysis. By doing this, the marketer can judge each marketing program on its own merits and on the basis of whether it will contribute to help cover the company's fixed costs.

The short-term objective is to make sure the marketing programs generate enough sales to adequately cover the direct marketing costs necessary to generate the sales. The longer-term objective is to develop programs that cover both direct marketing costs and fixed overhead, resulting in a profit to the firm. Exhibit 17.2 provides a contribution to fixed costs payback example for a start-up direct mail/response program for an existing firm.

There are few limitations to this methodology for most companies. However, the question of capacity must be addressed. If, for example, you brew beer and you are at full capacity, the marketer would need to make sure that the revenues from *all the marketing programs together* cover both total variable marketing expenses and total fixed overhead. However, unless there is the issue of full capacity, *individual marketing programs* should normally be judged only on their ability to cover variable expenses and contribute to fixed overhead. The overhead will be there whether the program is executed or not. Thus, *if there is excess capacity,* it is always better to execute an additional program that covers the variable costs associated with the program and will contribute some additional revenue toward covering some of the fixed costs.

The payback analysis shown in Exhibit 17.3 is for a retail chain's annual marketing plan. (A worksheet is provided at the end of this chapter.) The analysis determines whether projected sales will cover marketing expenditures, allowing for a contribution to fixed costs and overhead.

Gross Margin to Net Sales Payback Analysis

With package goods marketers, payback calculations are sometimes analyzed slightly differently than for retailers. The gross margin often is defined as covering advertising, promotion, and profit and is referred to as gross margin to net sales or sometimes as advertising, promotion, and profit (AP&P). For example, if there is a 40 percent gross margin, 40 percent of all sales would cover advertising and promotion costs (consumer and trade) and

**EXHIBIT 17.2   Contribution to Fixed Overhead Payback Analysis for a
Direct Response Marketing Program**

	Estimated Response		
	Low	Medium	High
Projected Mailing to 10,000 Customers	1 Percent	2.5 Percent	5 Percent
Responses	100	250	500
Gross sales ($26 per order)	$2,600	$6,500	$13,000
Less refunds (5 percent of sales)	130	325	650
Less cancellations (2 percent of sales)	52	130	260
Net sales	2,418	6,045	12,090
Less cost of goods sold (40 percent)	967	2,418	4,836
Gross profit	1,451	3,627	7,254
Less selling expense			
Catalog production mailing			
(@ 20 cents per piece)	2,000	2,000	2,000
List rental	N/C	N/C	N/C
Photography	N/C	N/C	N/C
Type	N/C	N/C	N/C
Boxes, forms, supplies (2 percent of gross)	52	130	260
Order processing ($3.20/order)	320	800	1,600
Return postage	N/C	N/C	N/C
Telephone	10	10	10
Credit card (30 percent credit card sales with 3 percent charge from store's bank)	23	59	117
Total Expenses	$2,405	$2,999	$3,987
Contribution to Fixed Costs	$ (954)	$ 626	$3,267

**EXHIBIT 17.3   Contribution to Fixed Overhead Payback Analysis for a
Retail Marketing Plan**

Assumptions
The plan will result in a 10 percent store-for-store increase in sales over last year.
Cost of goods sold will average 50 percent throughout the year.

Nine stores	$M	$M
Sales	$7,920.0	
Less cost of goods sold	3,960.0	
Gross profit		$3,960.0
Less:		
Media	$ 316.8	
Production costs	31.7	
Promotion costs	50.0	
Merchandising	30.0	
Selling	25.0	
Research	20.0	
Public relations/miscellaneous	5.0	
Total marketing mix tools		478.5
Contribution to fixed costs		$3,481.5
Fixed costs		3,081.5
Profit before taxes		$ 400.0

EXHIBIT 17.4   Gross Margin to Net Sales Payback Analysis for a New Package Goods Product

Assumptions:
$100MM product category, with growth rate of 10 percent per year.
Three competing brands in the category and miscellaneous private labels.
Introduction of new product at an expected margin of 40 percent.

	Year 1 Projections	Year 2 Projections	Year 3 Projections
Net sales	$10.0MM	$12.0MM	$13.0MM
Gross margin (40%)	4.0	4.8	5.2
Less promotion	3.0	2.5	1.5
Less advertising	2.0	1.5	1.5
Profit/(loss)	(1.0)	0.8	2.2

provide the profit. Furthermore, 60 percent of the sales would cover all allocated fixed costs (plant, equipment, etc.) as well as the variable selling costs (selling costs, salaries, raw material, product manufacturing cost, etc.).

The example shown in Exhibit 17.4 utilizes the gross margin to net sales payback methodology. We are assuming a 40 percent margin on a new product. The payback analysis is projected for three years in order to determine both the short-term and the longer-term profitability for the new product. In this example, the product is projected to payback sometime early in year three. (A worksheet is provided at the end of this chapter.)

MARKETING CALENDAR OVERVIEW

After the marketing plan budget and payback have been completed, it is time to summarize the plan on a single page. This summary should be in the form of a marketing calendar. When completed, the marketing calendar will serve as a visual summary of the marketing plan for the specific designated period or, more likely, the coming year.

A marketing calendar should contain the following elements:

- Headings, including product/service/store name, time period, date prepared, and a geographic reference (national, regional, group of markets or tier) or individual market name

- A visual summary of the marketing program week by week or month by month, outlining all marketing tool executions and including all other marketing related activities, such as research

- A visual summary of media weight levels by week

Prepare a separate marketing calendar if there are substantial geographic differences by region or market and also for test markets. Exhibit 17.5 shows a prototype for you to follow when developing your own marketing calendar. A retail chain plan is used for the example. A blank calendar is provided at the end of this chapter.

EXHIBIT 17.5   Example of a Marketing Calendar

1993 National Marketing Calendar

HEARTLAND

DECEMBER 1, 1992

Monday (Bdcst) Dates

Media	JAN	FEB	MAR	APR	MAY	JUN	JUL	AUG	SEP	OCT	NOV	DEC
	28 4 11 18 25	1 8 15 22	1 8 15 22	29 5 12 19	26 3 10 17 24 31	7 14 21	28 5 12 19	26 2 9 16 23 30	6 13 20	27 4 11 18 25	1 8 15 22 29	6 13 20

MARKETING PROGRAMS

- Mainline Promotions — MAINLINE (FEB–MAR), MAINLINE (MAY–JUN), MAINLINE (AUG–SEP)
- Clearance Sale — CLEARANCE (JAN), CLEARANCE (JUL)
- Half Price Sale — HALF PRICE (APR)
- Anniversary Sale — ANNIVERSARY (OCT)
- Price/Item and Thanksgiving Sale — THANKSGIVING (NOV)
- Holiday Sale — HOLIDAY (DEC)

MEDIA ACTIVITIES

- Television 50% :30's/50% :10's
- 7 Weeks at 200 GRP's
- Newspaper 1/3 page ads — 12 Times
- Newspaper 1/4 page ads — 12 Times
- Direct Mail – 4 Mailings — 10,000 Per Store, Per Mailing

NON-MEDIA ACTIVITIES

- Point-of-Purchase Displays
- In-Store Signage
- In-Store Seminars
- Promotion P-O-P
- Research — Market and In-Store
- In-Store Price Promotion
- Red Tag Sale
- In-Store Volume Discount
- Promotion and Gift Wrapping

Worksheet 17.1   Marketing Budget

	($M)	Percent of Total Budget

Marketing Mix Tool

Media
    Television
    Newspaper
    Radio
    Direct mail
    Outdoor
    Other
    Total
Production
    Television
    Newspaper
    Radio
    Direct mail
    Outdoor
    Other
    Total
Product/Branding/Packaging
    Total
Personal Selling/Operations
    Total
Promotion
    Redemption cost
    Media support
    Production
    Total
Merchandising
    Production
    Total
Publicity
    Total
Research
    Total
Miscellaneous
    Total
Grand Total

Total Budget Compared to Industry Average and Previous Year
Marketing as a percent of sales per plan.
Marketing as a percent of sales per industry average.
Index company budget to industry average.
Index company budget to previous year.

Total Planned Budget Compared to Competition
Total planned budget for company.
Total estimated budget for Competitor A.
Total estimated budget for Competitor B.
Total estimated budget for Competitor C.

Worksheet 17.2   Contribution to Fixed Overhead

Payback Analysis

Assumptions

Sales
Less cost of goods sold
    Gross profit
Less:
    Media
    Production costs
    Promotions costs
    Merchandising
    Selling
    Research
    Public relations/miscellaneous

Total marketing mix tools

Contribution to fixed costs
Fixed costs
Profit before taxes

Worksheet 17.3   Gross Margin to Net Sales

Payback Analysis

Assumptions

	Year 1 Projections	Year 2 Projections	Year 3 Projections
Net sales			
Gross margin			
Less promotion			
Less advertising			
Profit/(loss)			

Worksheet 17.4

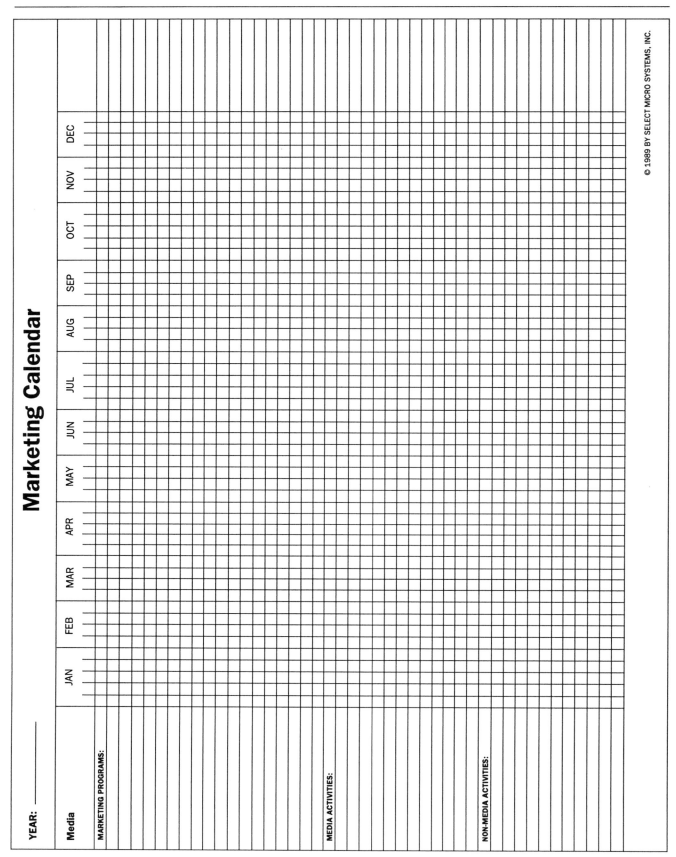

Marketing Calendar

YEAR: _____

Media	JAN	FEB	MAR	APR	MAY	JUN	JUL	AUG	SEP	OCT	NOV	DEC

MARKETING PROGRAMS:

MEDIA ACTIVITIES:

NON-MEDIA ACTIVITIES:

STEP NINE | Execution

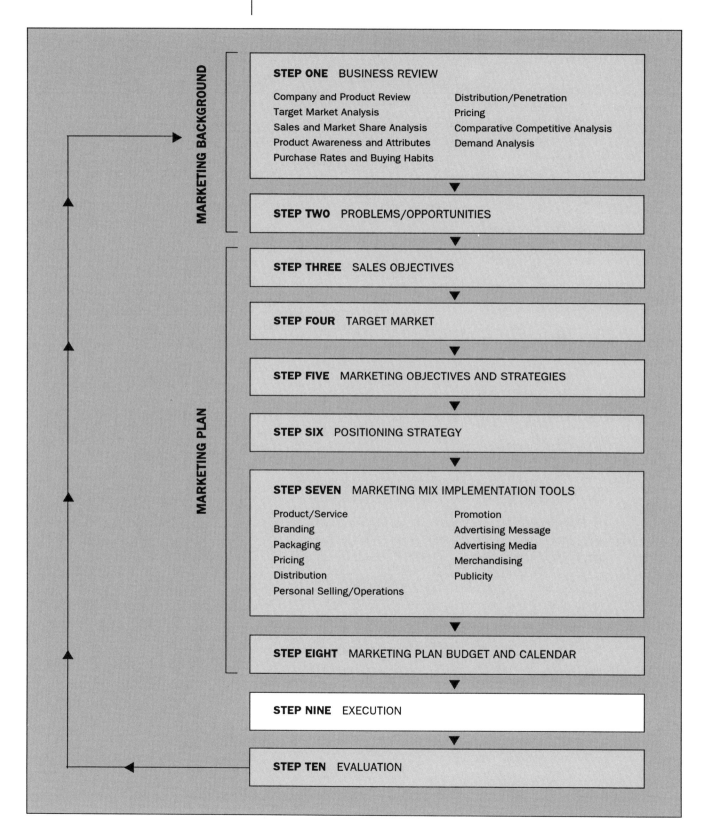

MARKETING BACKGROUND

STEP ONE   BUSINESS REVIEW

Company and Product Review	Distribution/Penetration
Target Market Analysis	Pricing
Sales and Market Share Analysis	Comparative Competitive Analysis
Product Awareness and Attributes	Demand Analysis
Purchase Rates and Buying Habits	

STEP TWO   PROBLEMS/OPPORTUNITIES

MARKETING PLAN

STEP THREE   SALES OBJECTIVES

STEP FOUR   TARGET MARKET

STEP FIVE   MARKETING OBJECTIVES AND STRATEGIES

STEP SIX   POSITIONING STRATEGY

STEP SEVEN   MARKETING MIX IMPLEMENTATION TOOLS

Product/Service	Promotion
Branding	Advertising Message
Packaging	Advertising Media
Pricing	Merchandising
Distribution	Publicity
Personal Selling/Operations	

STEP EIGHT   MARKETING PLAN BUDGET AND CALENDAR

STEP NINE   EXECUTION

STEP TEN   EVALUATION

EXECUTING THE PLAN
IN THE MARKETPLACE

Once the marketing plan is finally completed,
you will execute the plan in the marketplace.

Evaluation

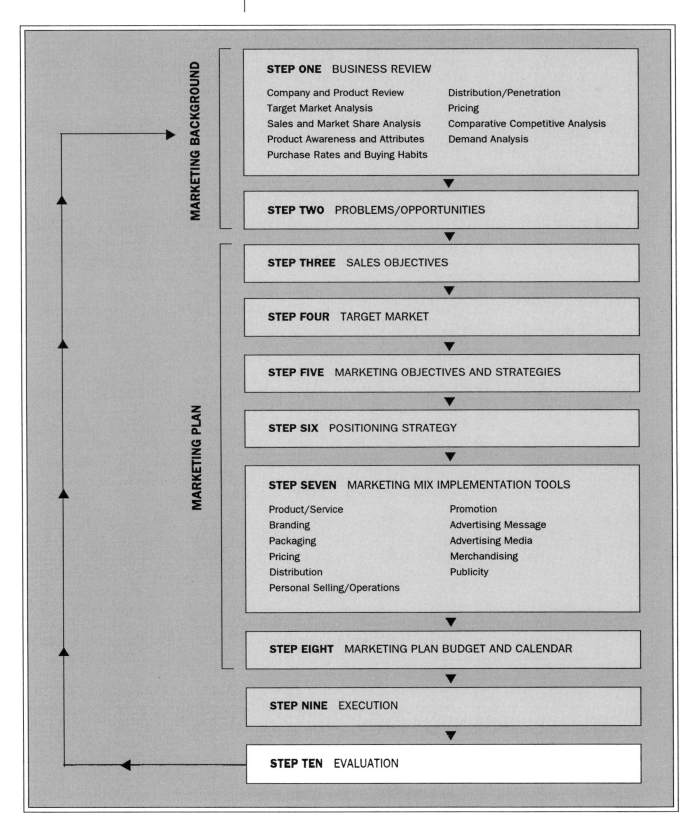

MARKETING BACKGROUND

STEP ONE BUSINESS REVIEW

Company and Product Review
Target Market Analysis
Sales and Market Share Analysis
Product Awareness and Attributes
Purchase Rates and Buying Habits

Distribution/Penetration
Pricing
Comparative Competitive Analysis
Demand Analysis

STEP TWO PROBLEMS/OPPORTUNITIES

MARKETING PLAN

STEP THREE SALES OBJECTIVES

STEP FOUR TARGET MARKET

STEP FIVE MARKETING OBJECTIVES AND STRATEGIES

STEP SIX POSITIONING STRATEGY

STEP SEVEN MARKETING MIX IMPLEMENTATION TOOLS

Product/Service
Branding
Packaging
Pricing
Distribution
Personal Selling/Operations

Promotion
Advertising Message
Advertising Media
Merchandising
Publicity

STEP EIGHT MARKETING PLAN BUDGET AND CALENDAR

STEP NINE EXECUTION

STEP TEN EVALUATION

18

Evaluation

After the "in the marketplace execution" of your marketing plan, you need to evaluate the results. An evaluation methodology should be established to assure ongoing evaluation of the marketing plan executions. This information will provide invaluable feedback from which to make modifications during the year. It will also provide a database from which to make strategic decisions that have impact on the following year's plan.

OVERVIEW

Upon completion of specific marketing activities, such as an individual advertising campaign, a promotion, a pricing change, a media test, or a year-long plan, there should be an evaluation of the results. In addition, every objective in your marketing plan should be used as a measuring tool for evaluation. To help in the evaluation process, we have included different evaluation methods.

COMPARATIVE AND SALES TREND METHOD

This sales evaluation method analyzes current sales with the previous year's sales *before, during,* and *after* any given marketing execution. Sales are analyzed before the promotion period to determine if there was a downward, upward, or flat sales trend compared to the previous year's sales. Sales are also compared in this same manner to last year's, both during and after the execution period. In analyzing the *preperiod,* the *execution period,* and the *postperiod* separately, added insight is provided on the effect of the individual test or marketing execution. Sales might have been trending down prior to the marketing execution. Even a small increase during the marketing execution period would mean that the marketing execution might have helped reverse a negative trend. Then, in analyzing sales after the marketing execution period, the marketer can begin to determine whether the marketing execution had any long-term effect on sales. If the marketing execution was designed to gain new users or trial of the product, the sales results in the months after the execution will help determine whether repeat purchase or continuity of purchase was achieved.

There are two sales trending methods: sales trending analysis with control markets and without control markets.

Sales Trending Analysis with Control Markets

This methodology utilizes control markets (markets with no marketing execution or markets receiving a mainline marketing execution) to compare against test markets receiving a new marketing execution or the marketing execution you want to analyze. Control and test markets should be similar in terms of sales volume, sales trending, distribution levels, penetration/marketing coverage, size, demographic profile, and other market and media characteristics. Also, there should be a minimum of two test and two control markets to guard against any anomalies.

In summary, control markets allow for a benchmark on whether the specific marketing execution was responsible for sales increases in the test markets. If the analysis demonstrates that sales and profits in test markets which received advertising were substantially above control markets which received no advertising, then the decision should be made to consider rolling out advertising to other markets.

Sales Trending Analysis without Control Markets

Whenever possible, we recommend using the sales trending analysis with control markets. However, for many businesses, control markets are not available because the business is located solely in one market or in a minimal number of markets. In other situations, the marketer needs to analyze results of a marketing execution that was implemented across all markets. In these situations, a sales trending analysis without control markets is used. Sales are analyzed before, during, and after the execution to determine if the period during the marketing execution received greater total sales and greater percentage sales increases or decreases over last year. Without control markets, the marketer can't be sure that the sales results are totally a function of the marketing execution. The results could be the effect of other market factors, which caused marketwide sales increases or decreases for not only your company but for the competition as well. However, even without control markets, the sales trending analysis provides general insight into the success or failure of individual marketing executions.

Sometimes test market performance is compared to national or total company sales. In this case, the national or company total is used as a benchmark. The method is not as accurate as test versus control market evaluation, but it does provide a basis for comparison.

PRE- AND POST-RESEARCH

Pre- and postmarket primary research is implemented both before and after the execution of the plan. Most pre- and postresearch involves awareness, attitude, and behavior tracking studies. These studies monitor the movement of awareness, attitude, and behavior variables both before and after the marketing execution.

While increased sales is a very valuable indicator of the success of a marketing execution, it is not the only one. Many times while sales remain relatively flat, there is a significant movement in awareness and attitudes. These shifts signal the probability of future increases in sales. As has been

EXHIBIT 18.1 Advertising Awareness/Attitude Indices

	No Advertising Control Markets			Advertising Test Markets			Net Gain
	Pre	Post	Difference	Pre	Post	Difference	
Advertising awareness	(100)	(105)	+5	(100)	(152)	+52	+47
Better source of energy information	(100)	(82)	−18	(100)	(135)	+35	+53
More concerned about energy conservation	(100)	(84)	−16	(100)	(127)	+27	+43
More concerned with the environment	(100)	(100)	—	(100)	(115)	+15	+15

proven time and time again, with increase in awareness there is a good probability that there will be an increased level of purchases.

Pre- and postresearch can also serve as a diagnostic tool to help explain why sales went up or down. Research can uncover changes in consumer awareness of your product, attitudes about your product, changing purchase behavior patterns, or competitive strengths and weaknesses as reasons for increases or decreases in sales. Thus, the research evaluation method has the capability of providing more in-depth information than the sales trending method.

In summary, research allows the marketer to evaluate the success or failure of marketing and communication programs. Research can help you determine whether you met your advertising objectives of "increasing awareness from 50 percent to 60 percent" and "improving the quality ratings of your product." In addition, research can help evaluate the success of other such marketing objectives as "increasing the sales ratio (percentage of customers shopping who make a purchase) from 30 percent to 40 percent." Above all, research is an evaluation tool that lets you determine why your sales goals were or were not achieved.

The example in Exhibit 18.1 demonstrates the ability of pre- and post-research to evaluate the results of an advertising program. In this example, a utility was evaluating the effectiveness of its campaign to persuade consumers that it was a better source of energy information and more concerned about energy conservation and environmental issues. The numbers have been indexed for confidentiality. The results clearly provided the utility with insights into the effectiveness of the campaign.

GROWTH RATE OF IMPROVEMENT SALES TRENDING MODEL

The growth rate of improvement sales trending model demonstrates how to measure your marketing activities. A retail example is used; however, a similar procedure could be established for any business type. The only changes needed to make the model applicable to any business would be in the evaluation categories. These would be made consistent with the business. A manufacturer would use product sales and units sold. A retailer could use such measurements as visits, transactions, dollars per transaction, units sold, and product sales. And a service firm would use sales and people served.

You should plan to use a similar method for your evaluation system. A worksheet is provided at the end of this chapter. However, wherever appropriate, we suggest that the pre- and postresearch evaluation method also be utilized and that the research be executed by a professional research firm. The following provides an example of an evaluation objective and strategies along with an execution format for the growth rate of improvement sales trending evaluation process.

Evaluation Objective

Develop a data feedback methodology to monitor and determine results of marketing test strategies and executions.

Evaluation Strategies

Implement a disciplined data feedback system in order to quickly and easily evaluate sales activity for marketing planning and execution.

Utilize the growth rate of improvement (GRI) method.

Execution

Each *test market* is compared with a *control market* of similar type and number of stores and per store sales averages. The test markets receive the test activity, and the control markets receive the regularly scheduled marketing activity. If you don't have control markets, the test market can be compared against your national system or all other markets.

Step 1. A *preperiod* is analyzed to determine sales trending prior to the test period.

Step 2. For the *test period,* the period during which the marketing program is executed, data are analyzed to determine sales trending.

Step 3. For the *postperiod,* the period immediately following a test period, data are analyzed to determine sales trending.

Step 4. Finally a *growth rate of improvement* is analyzed by determining the difference between visits, transactions, and sales dollars per store in the preperiod, the test period, and the postperiod. The data enables the marketer to determine incremental visits, transactions, and sales during the test period for each market and to evaluate the rate of success.

Whenever feasible, you should utilize the growth rate improvement method to compare the preperiod to the test period, test period to postperiod, and the preperiod to the postperiod. The preperiod is compared to the test to determine if the test altered expected behavior. If the preperiod showed sales were flat, and the test period demonstrated a marked increase in sales, a determination would be made that the marketing program executed during the test period was effective. The test period is compared to the postperiod to determine whether the marketing execution had a lasting effect and to gain knowledge on how much, if any, sales drop off occurred after the test period.

Finally, a very important long-term analysis is the preperiod comparison to the postperiod. This comparison shows whether the marketing execution had a positive effect on sales after the test as compared to sales trending before the marketing execution or test period.

Examples of Preperiod to Test Period Comparisons

Two examples demonstrate a preperiod comparison to test period. Exhibit 18.2 compares a test market to a control market and Exhibit 18.3 compares a test market to the national system average.

**EXHIBIT 18.2   Test versus Control Market Dollar Sales Analysis:
Test Period 2/24 to 3/30 (Weekly per Store Average)**

	Last Year Dollars (000)	This Year Dollars (000)	Percent Change Dollars
Preperiod 1/20-2/23			
Test market—Detroit (2 Stores)	$121.0	$185.1	+53%
Control market—Indianapolis (2 Stores)	118.0	159.3	+35
Test Period 2/24-2/30			
Test market—Detroit (2 Stores)	29.0	53.4	+84
Control market—Indianapolis (2 Stores)	26.0	25.7	-1

	Preperiod Percent Change	Test Period Percent Change	Percent Point Gain/Loss
Growth Rate Improvement (GRI)			
Test market—Detroit (2 Stores)	+53%	+84%	+31%
Control market—Indianapolis (2 Stores)	+35	−1	−36
Net percent point difference	+18%	+85%	+67%

Incremental Sales:
GRI: +67 percent x Test period Sales $53,400 = Net Weekly Gain $35,778

Note: The same method would be used for visits and/or transactions if the data are available.

**EXHIBIT 18.3   Test versus National Dollar Sales Analysis:
Test Period 2/24 to 3/30 (Weekly per Store Average)**

	Last Year Dollars (000)	This Year Dollars (000)	Percent Change Dollars
Preperiod 1/20-2/23			
Test market—Detroit (2 Stores)	$121.0	$185.1	+53%
National system average	120.0	144.0	+20
Test Period 2/24-2/30			
Test market—Detroit (2 Stores)	29.0	53.4	+84
National system average	27.0	31.6	+17

	Preperiod Percent Change	Test Period Percent Change	Percent Point Gain/Loss
Growth Rate Improvement (GRI)			
Test market—Detroit (2 Stores)	+53%	+84%	+31%
National system average	+20	+17	−3
Net percent point difference	+33%	+67%	+34%

Incremental Sales:
GRI: + 34 percent x Test Period Sales $53,400 = Net Weekly Gain $18,156

Note: The same method would be used for visits and/or transactions if the data are available.

Worksheet 18.1   Growth Rate of Improvement Sales Trending Model

Evaluation Objective

Evaluation Strategies

Evaluation Execution

Test Market versus Control Market Dollar Sales Analysis

Test Period _____

	Last Year $	This Year $	Percent Change
Preperiod versus	Preperiod		
Test Period _____	Test market		
	Control market		
	Test period		
	Test market		
	Control market		

Growth Rate Improvement	Preperiod Percent Change	Test Period Percent Change	Point Gain/Loss
Test market			
Control market			
Net percent point difference			

Incremental sales: GRI _____ x Test Period Sales $ _____ = Net Weekly Gain $ _____

	Last Year $	This Year $	Percent Change
Test Period versus	Test period		
Postperiod _____	Test market		
	Control market		
	Postperiod		
	Test market		
	Control market		

Growth Rate of Improvement Sales Trending Model (Continued)

Growth Rate Improvement	Test Period Percent Change	Postperiod Percent Change	Point Gain/Loss
Test market			
Control market			
Net percent point difference			

Incremental sales: GRI _____ x Test Period Sales $ _____ = Net Weekly Gain $ _____

	Last Year	This Year	Percent Change

Postperiod versus Preperiod _____

	Last Year	This Year	Percent Change
Postperiod			
Test market			
Control market			
Preperiod			
Test market			
Control market			

Growth Rate Improvement	Postperiod Percent Change	Preperiod Percent Change	Point Gain/Loss
Test market			
Control market			
Net percent point difference			

Incremental sales: GRI _____ x Test Period Sales $ _____ = Net Weekly Gain $ _____

Test Market versus National System Average Dollar Sales Analysis

Test Period _____

	Last Year	This Year	Percent Change

Preperiod versus Test Period _____

	Last Year	This Year	Percent Change
Preperiod			
Test market			
National system average			
Test period			
Test market			
National system average			

Growth Rate Improvement	Preperiod Percent Change	Test Period Percent Change	Point Gain/Loss
Test market			
National system average			
Net percent point difference			

Incremental sales: GRI _____ x Test Period Sales $ _____ = Net Weekly Gain $ _____

Worksheet 18.1

	Last Year	This Year	Percent Change

**Test Period versus
Postperiod** _____

Test Period
   Test market
   National system average
Postperiod
   Test market
   National system average

Growth Rate Improvement	Test period Percent Change	Postperiod Percent Change	Point Gain/Loss

Test market
National system average
   Net percent point difference

Incremental sales: GRI _____ x Test Period Sales $ _____ = Net Weekly Gain $ _____

	Last Year	This Year	Percent Change

**Postperiod versus
Preperiod** _____

Postperiod
   Test market
   National system average
Preperiod
   Test market
   National system average

Growth Rate Improvement	Postperiod Percent Change	Preperiod Percent Change	Point Gain/Loss

Test market
National system average
   Net percent point difference

Incremental sales: GRI _____ x Test Period Sales $ _____ = Net Weekly Gain $ _____

Index